Lecture Notes in Computer Science 16156

Founding Editors

Gerhard Goos
Juris Hartmanis

The series Lecture Notes in Computer Science (LNCS), including its subseries Lecture Notes in Artificial Intelligence (LNAI) and Lecture Notes in Bioinformatics (LNBI), has established itself as a medium for the publication of new developments in computer science and information technology research, teaching, and education.

LNCS enjoys close cooperation with the computer science R & D community, the series counts many renowned academics among its volume editors and paper authors, and collaborates with prestigious societies. Its mission is to serve this international community by providing an invaluable service, mainly focused on the publication of conference and workshop proceedings and postproceedings. LNCS commenced publication in 1973.

Yujiu Yang · Mengxing Huang · Xiuqin Pan ·
Jiajia Zhang · Junyang Chen · Liang-Jie Zhang
Editors

Cognitive Computing - ICCC 2025

9th International Conference
Held as Part of the Services Conference Federation, SCF 2025
Hong Kong, China, September 27–30, 2025
Proceedings

 Springer

Editors
Yujiu Yang
Tsinghua University
Shenzhen, China

Mengxing Huang
Hainan University
Haikou, China

Xiuqin Pan
Minzu University of China
Beijing, China

Jiajia Zhang
Harbin Institute of Technology
Shenzhen, China

Junyang Chen
Shenzhen University
Shenzhen, China

Liang-Jie Zhang ⓘ
Shenzhen University
Shenzhen, China

ISSN 0302-9743   ISSN 1611-3349 (electronic)
Lecture Notes in Computer Science
ISBN 978-3-032-06309-0   ISBN 978-3-032-06310-6 (eBook)
https://doi.org/10.1007/978-3-032-06310-6

This Springer imprint is published by the registered company Springer Nature Switzerland AG
The registered company address is: Gewerbestrasse 11, 6330 Cham, Switzerland

If disposing of this product, please recycle the paper.

Preface

The 2025 International Conference on Cognitive Computing (ICCC) aimed to cover all aspects of Sensing Intelligence (SI) as a Service (SIaaS). Cognitive Computing is a sensing-driven-computing (SDC) scheme that explores and integrates intelligence from all types of senses in various scenarios and solution contexts. It goes well beyond the five normal human senses, which consist of four major senses (sight, smell, hearing, and taste) located in specific parts of the body, as well as a sense of touch located all over the body.

ICCC 2025 was a member of the Services Conference Federation (SCF). SCF 2025 had the following 10 collocated service-oriented sister conferences: 2025 International Conference on Web Services (ICWS 2025), 2025 International Conference on Cloud Computing (CLOUD 2025), 2025 International Conference on Services Computing (SCC 2025), 2025 International Conference on Big Data (BigData 2025), 2025 International Conference on AI and Multimodal Services (AIMS 2025), 2025 International Conference on Metaverse (METAVERSE 2025), 2025 International Conference on Internet of Things (ICIOT 2025), 2025 International Conference on Cognitive Computing (ICCC 2025), 2025 International Conference on Edge Computing (EDGE 2025), and 2025 International Conference on Blockchain (ICBC 2025). As the founding member of SCF, the first International Conference on Web Services (ICWS) was held in June 2003 in Las Vegas, USA. Meanwhile, the First International Conference on Web Services - Europe 2003 (ICWS-Europe 2003) was held in Germany in October, 2003. ICWS-Europe 2003 was an extended event of the 2003 International Conference on Web Services (ICWS 2003) in Europe. In 2004, ICWS-Europe was changed to the European Conference on Web Services (ECOWS), which was held at Erfurt, Germany.

This volume presents the accepted papers of the 2025 International Conference on Cognitive Computing (ICCC 2025), held in Hong Kong, China during September 27–30, 2025. For this conference, each paper was single-blind reviewed by two or three independent members of the International Program Committee. After carefully evaluating their originality and quality, we accepted 7 papers from 11 submissions.

We are pleased to thank the authors whose submissions and participation made this conference possible. We also want to express our thanks to the Organizing Committee and Program Committee members, for their dedication in helping to organize the conference and reviewing the submissions. We owe special thanks to the keynote speakers for their impressive speeches.

Finally, we would like to thank operations team members Jing Zeng, Sheng He, Yishuang Ning, and Zhuolin Mei, for their excellent work in organizing this conference.

We look forward to your future great contributions as a volunteer, author, and conference participant in the fast-growing worldwide services innovations community.

September 2025

Yujiu Yang
Mengxing Huang
Xiuqin Pan
Jiajia Zhang
Junyang Chen
Liang-Jie Zhang

Organization

Program Chairs

Yujiu Yang	Tsinghua University, China
Mengxing Huang	Hainan University, China
Xiuqin Pan	Minzu University of China, China
Jiajia Zhang	Harbin Institute of Technology, China
Junyang Chen	Shenzhen University, China

Services Conference Federation (SCF 2025)

General Chairs

Ali Arsanjani	Google, USA
Wu Chou	Essenlix Corporation, USA

Coordinating Program Chair

Liang-Jie Zhang	Shenzhen University, China

CFO and International Affairs Chair

Min Luo	Georgia Tech, USA

Operation Committee

Jing Zeng	China Gridcom Co., Ltd., China
Yishuang Ning	Tsinghua University, China
Sheng He	Kingdee International Software Group Co., Ltd., China
Zhuolin Mei	Jiujiang University, China

Steering Committee

Calton Pu (Co-chair)	Georgia Tech, USA
Liang-Jie Zhang (Co-chair)	Shenzhen University, China

ICCC 2025 Program Committee

Ting Jin	Hainan University, China
Nagarajan Kandasamy	Drexel University, USA
Ye Liu	Chinese Academy of Sciences, China
Lu Min	Shenzhen University, China
Rui André Oliveira	University of Lisbon, Portugal
Dwith Chenna	AMD, USA
M. Emre Gursoy	Koç University, Turkey
Peng Xu	Northeast Normal University, China
Limin Su	Beijing Union University, China
Liuqing Chen	Zhejiang University, China
Carson K. Leung	University of Manitoba, Canada
Supratik Mukhopadhyay	Louisiana State University, USA
Dong Wen	University of Science and Technology Beijing, China
Yi Zhou	University of Science and Technology Beijing, China

Conference Sponsor – Services Society

The Services Society (S2) is a non-profit professional organization that has been created to promote worldwide research and technical collaboration in services innovations among academia and industrial professionals. Its members are volunteers from industry and academia with common interests. S2 is registered in the USA as a "501(c) organization", which means that it is an American tax-exempt nonprofit organization. S2 collaborates with other professional organizations to sponsor or co-sponsor conferences and to promote an effective services curriculum in colleges and universities. S2 initiates and promotes a "Services University" program worldwide to bridge the gap between industrial needs and university instruction.

The Services Sector accounted for 79.5% of the GDP of the USA in 2016. The Services Society has formed 5 Special Interest Groups (SIGs) to support technology- and domain-specific professional activities.

- Special Interest Group on Services Computing (SIG-SC)
- Special Interest Group on Big Data (SIG-BD)
- Special Interest Group on Cloud Computing (SIG-CLOUD)
- Special Interest Group on Artificial Intelligence (SIG-AI)
- Special Interest Group on Metaverse (SIG-Metaverse)

About the Services Conference Federation (SCF)

As the founding member of the Services Conference Federation (SCF), the first **International Conference on Web Services (ICWS)** was held in June 2003 in Las Vegas, USA. Meanwhile, the First International Conference on Web Services - Europe 2003 (ICWS-Europe 2003) was held in Germany in October 2003. ICWS-Europe 2003 was an extended event of the 2003 International Conference on Web Services (ICWS 2003) in Europe. In 2004, ICWS-Europe was changed to the European Conference on Web Services (ECOWS), which was held in Erfurt, Germany.

Sponsored by the Services Society and Springer, SCF 2018 and SCF 2019 were held successfully on June 25 – June 30, 2018, in Seattle, USA, and on June 25 – June 30, 2019, in San Diego, USA. SCF 2020 and SCF 2021 were held successfully online and in satellite sessions in Shenzhen, China. SCF 2022 and 2023 were held successfully on December 10–14, 2022 and on September 23–26, 2023, in Hawaii, USA. SCF 2024 was held successfully on November 16–19, 2024, in Bangkok, Thailand. To celebrate its 23rd birthday, SCF 2025 was held on September 27–30, 2025, in Hong Kong, China.

In the past 22 years, the ICWS community has expanded from Web engineering innovations to scientific research for the whole services industry. Service delivery platforms have been expanded to mobile platforms, the Internet of Things, cloud computing, and edge computing. The services ecosystem has gradually been enabled, value-added, and intelligence embedded through enabling technologies such as big data, artificial intelligence, and cognitive computing. In the coming years, all transactions with multiple parties involved will be transformed into blockchain and metaverse.

Based on technology trends and best practices in the field, the Services Conference Federation (SCF) will continue serving as the conference umbrella's code name for all services-related conferences. SCF 2025 defined the future of New ABCDE (AI, Blockchain, Cloud, BigData, & IOT) and entered the 5G for Services Era. **The theme of SCF 2025 was Services Agent.** We are very proud to announce that SCF 2025's 10 co-located theme topic conferences all centered around "services", with each focusing on exploring different themes (web-based services, cloud-based services, Big Data-based services, services innovation lifecycle, AI-driven ubiquitous services, blockchain-driven trust service ecosystems, industry-specific services and applications, and emerging service-oriented technologies).

– **Bigger Platform:** The 10 collocated conferences (SCF 2025) were sponsored by the Services Society, which is the world-leading not-for-profit organization (501(c)(3)) dedicated to the service of more than 30,000 worldwide Services Computing researchers and practitioners. A bigger platform means bigger opportunities for all volunteers, authors, and participants. Meanwhile, Springer provided sponsorship of the best paper awards and other professional activities. All the 10 conference proceedings of SCF 2025 were published by Springer and indexed in the ISI Conference

Proceedings Citation Index (included in Web of Science), Engineering Index EI (Compendex and Inspec databases), DBLP, Google Scholar, IO-Port, MathSciNet, Scopus, and ZBlMath.

- **Brighter Future:** While celebrating the 2025 version of ICWS, SCF 2025 highlighted the International Conference on AI and Multimodal Services (AIMS 2025) to build the fundamental infrastructure for enabling AIGC services ecosystems. It will also lead our community members to create their own brighter future.
- **Better Model:** SCF 2025 continued to leverage the invented Conference Blockchain Model (CBM) to innovate the organizing practices for all the 10 theme conferences. Senior researchers in the field are welcome to submit proposals to serve as CBM Ambassador for an individual conference to start better interactions during your leadership role in organizing future SCF conferences.

We look forward to your great contributions as a volunteer, author, and conference participant for the fast-growing worldwide services innovations community. If you would like to contribute to SCF 2026 as a leading volunteer or try the new Conference Blockchain Model, please feel free to contact us to become a conference volunteer. For other queries or questions, please feel free to visit our conference websites and find contact information on SCF 2026.

All the invited talks and paper presentations of SCF 2020, SCF 2021, and SCF 2022 are open to all Services Society community members for free. You can watch all presentations through SCF 365.

Contents

Research Track

A Multimodal Retrieval-Augmented Generation System for Intelligent Question Answering

Bo Liu[1,2], Yishuang Ning[2], Sheng He[2], Fei Guo[1], Siyu Jia[2], and Li Zhu[1(✉)]

[1] School of Software Engineering, Xi'an Jiaotong University, Xi'an 710000, China
{boliu,co.fly}@stu.xjtu.edu.cn, zhuli@xjtu.edu.cn
[2] Kingdee International Software Group, Shenzhen 518057, China
{yishuang_ning,sheng_he,siyu_jia}@kingdee.com

Abstract. With the rapid advancement of multimodal large models, there is an increasing demand for intelligent question-answering systems capable of comprehending and leveraging complex, heterogeneous, and multi-source knowledge. However, existing approaches often face challenges in semantic alignment, efficient retrieval, and coherent generation, particularly when processing unstructured multimodal data and multi-turn dialogues. To address these limitations, this study presents a systematically designed multimodal retrieval-augmented generation (RAG) system that integrates advanced knowledge segmentation, hybrid retrieval, and generation techniques. In the offline stage, the system performs fine-grained knowledge segmentation and structured annotation through multimodal understanding, while enhancing global retrieval performance via multi-dimensional knowledge augmentation. In the online stage, it establishes an end-to-end, closed-loop answering pipeline that incorporates multi-turn dialogue rewriting, hybrid retrieval, reranking, and large model generation. Furthermore, a comprehensive automatic evaluation framework is developed to assess the system across multiple dimensions, including retrieval accuracy, factual consistency, generation quality, and structural clarity. Experimental results show that the proposed system substantially improves retrieval hit rates and generation performance over baseline methods. Overall, this work demonstrates the effectiveness of integrating RAG frameworks with multimodal large models and provides a solid foundation for deployment in high-demand domains such as healthcare, finance, and education.

Keywords: retrieval-augmented generation · multimodal · large models

1 Introduction

With the continuous advancement of artificial intelligence, intelligent question-answering systems have become a key means of information acquisition, demonstrating substantial application potential in domains such as healthcare [1], education [2], finance [3], and law [4]. Traditional text-based question-answering

Y. Yang et al. (Eds.): ICCC 2025, LNCS 16156, pp. 3–19, 2026.
https://doi.org/10.1007/978-3-032-06310-6_1

models exhibit notable limitations in understanding complex scenarios and integrating multi-source heterogeneous information, thus falling short of meeting the evolving demands for accuracy and richness. The emergence of multimodal generation technologies has revitalized intelligent question-answering systems by organically integrating diverse data types—such as text, images, and tables—thereby greatly expanding the scope of information retrieval and knowledge representation. In particular, when tasks require the interpretation of charts or visual content, or the fusion of structured and unstructured information for integrated output, multimodal approaches offer distinct advantages.

Retrieval-Augmented Generation (RAG) technology, as a significant breakthrough in contemporary generative artificial intelligence, provides an effective solution to inherent limitations of Large Language Models (LLMs), such as outdated knowledge and inconsistencies between generated content and the most recent facts [5]. By incorporating accurately retrieved information from external knowledge bases into the generation process, RAG not only enhances the authoritativeness of responses but also substantially improves their reliability in practical applications. For instance, research by AWS has shown that RAG systems enable LLMs to efficiently access extensive domain-specific data [6], dynamically expanding their knowledge scope without retraining. Similarly, NVIDIA has highlighted the promising potential of RAG methods in multimodal data processing [7]; the integration of tables, images, and complex charts broadens knowledge coverage and improves generative output quality [8].

Despite these promising prospects, applying RAG to multimodal intelligent question answering still faces critical challenges. First, semantic alignment across heterogeneous modalities remains a fundamental bottleneck: unlike textual data, modalities such as images and tables lack natural correspondence with language, making unified semantic representation and fusion particularly difficult [9,10]. Second, cross-modal retrieval requires a deep understanding of user intent and the ability to locate semantically relevant content from multi-source data, which involves complex tasks such as imagetext mapping, feature aggregation, and similarity modeling. Third, during generation, systems often struggle to balance multimodal information, minimize redundancy, and maintain factual consistency—especially when confronted with noisy or overlapping retrieved content.

To address these challenges, this paper proposes a multimodal RAG system tailored for intelligent question-answering scenarios. In the offline stage, the system performs fine-grained knowledge segmentation, structured annotation, and multi-dimensional knowledge enhancement to enable precise representation and indexing of multimodal content. In the online stage, we design a closed-loop pipeline that integrates multi-turn dialogue rewriting, hybrid retrieval, reranking, and large language modelbased generation. These components operate in synergy to achieve accurate cross-modal understanding, efficient retrieval, and controllable response generation.

Based on this framework, we implement a complete end-to-end multimodal RAG system and apply it to a variety of intelligent question-answering tasks involving complex inputs such as financial reports and images.

The main contributions of this study are as follows:

- Proposes innovative and systematically evaluated retrieval strategies for intelligent question answering, providing a comprehensive analysis and validation of retrieval performance across diverse scenarios, and clarifying efficient integration pathways between current mainstream large models and retrieval mechanisms.
- Conducts in-depth analysis of advanced textual content combination methods and key technical routes for multimodal data understanding and fusion, introducing a multimodal information processing framework suitable for complex application scenarios.
- Develops an end-to-end evaluation system that fully leverages large model capabilities to enable automatic, multi-dimensional, and objective assessment of system outputs, ensuring both the effectiveness and practical applicability of the model.

2   Related Work

Retrieval-Augmented Generation (RAG) systems integrate retrieval and generation components to enhance the factual accuracy and knowledge relevance of large language models. In the context of multimodal intelligent question answering, the overall performance of RAG systems critically depends on three aspects: the effectiveness of the retrieval mechanism, the quality of semantic alignment across heterogeneous modalities, and the expressive capacity of the generation model. This section surveys recent advances from four fundamental perspectives: (1) retrieval and indexing techniques within RAG frameworks, (2) multimodal semantic embedding and alignment strategies, (3) large language models tailored for multimodal understanding and generation, and (4) approaches to prompt engineering and retrieval optimization.

2.1   Retrieval Methods in RAG Frameworks

Contemporary RAG systems generally leverage dense retrieval, sparse retrieval, or hybrid retrieval approaches. Dense retrieval often relies on dual-encoder architectures trained with contrastive learning, enabling efficient and scalable retrieval. Meanwhile, traditional sparse retrieval techniques, such as BM25 [11], maintain competitive performance in scenarios demanding high precision. Hybrid retrieval methods combine the strengths of both dense and sparse retrieval, thereby enhancing coverage and robustness. For instance, the BGE-M3 model exemplifies this integration by supporting dense, sparse, and multi-vector retrieval tailored for high-dimensional multilingual documents [12]. Additionally, open-source re-rankers like bge-reranker-v2-m3 improve hybrid retrieval pipelines through fine-grained document scoring, further refining retrieval quality.

2.2   Multimodal Embedding and Semantic Alignment

Addressing the challenge of aligning heterogeneous modalities such as images, tables, and text, multimodal embedding models aim to project diverse inputs into a shared semantic space. The GME model [13], developed by Alibaba DAMO Academy, employs contrastive learning to achieve semantic alignment across modalities, using Qwen2-VL as the underlying backbone. This model is particularly effective for complex visual-text scenarios, such as financial reports, without dependence on optical character recognition (OCR). Such approaches have demonstrated substantial improvements in cross-modal and hybrid-modal retrieval performance.

2.3   Large Language Models for Multimodal Understanding and Text Generation

Large language models (LLMs) constitute the core component of retrieval-augmented generation systems, functioning as the backbone for answer synthesis. Within multimodal RAG systems, these models can be broadly categorized into two types: multimodal large language models (MLLMs), capable of directly processing and integrating inputs across multiple modalities, and text-based LLMs, which specialize in language understanding and generation.

Multimodal LLMs such as GPT-4o [14] and Qwen-VL [15] exhibit strong capabilities in handling visual, textual, and other forms of data. GPT-4o ("o" denoting omni-modality) represents OpenAI's first natively multimodal model, supporting inputs spanning text, images, audio, and video, while generating coherent outputs in both textual and auditory forms. It demonstrates notable improvements in visual reasoning tasks without compromising text generation quality. Similarly, Alibaba DAMO Academy's Qwen-VL-Plus and Qwen-VL-Max models provide enhanced high-resolution image understanding and fine-grained visual reasoning, rendering them particularly suitable for applications such as document parsing and table-based question answering.

Conversely, text-only LLMs—including GPT-4 [14] and the Qwen2/Qwen2.5 [16,17] series—remain dominant in pure language generation tasks. These models are typically employed within RAG architectures to generate final responses based on multimodal retrieval results. Their strengths lie in semantic comprehension, factual consistency, and logical coherence, making them well-suited for converting structured or semi-structured multimodal inputs into high-quality natural language answers. In multilingual and Chinese-language settings, the Qwen family demonstrates particularly strong performance, attributable to large-scale pretraining and domain-specific adaptation.

By leveraging the multimodal input processing capabilities of MLLMs alongside the expressive generation power of text-based LLMs, RAG systems can attain robust end-to-end performance in complex intelligent question answering scenarios.

2.4   Prompt Engineering and Retrieval Optimization

Prompt engineering plays a crucial role in enhancing the synergy between retrieval and generation components within RAG systems. Techniques such as structured prompting, few-shot exemplars, and instruction tuning effectively guide the generation process to better exploit retrieved contextual information [18]. On the retrieval front, multi-stage pipelines, embedding fine-tuning, and re-ranking strategies—exemplified by models like BGE-M3 and GME—substantially improve recall rates and reduce irrelevant noise. The joint optimization of retrieval mechanisms and prompt design is fundamental to achieving consistent and high-quality answer generation in both open-domain and domain-specific applications [19].

3   Methodology

3.1   Method Overview

To effectively support multimodal intelligent question answering, our system adopts a two-stage architecture comprising an offline knowledge preprocessing stage and an online answering stage. In the offline stage, raw documents are first segmented into fine-grained semantic chunks. Subsequently, a knowledge enhancement module enriches these chunks by generating additional semantically informative representations—such as summaries, tags, and entity links—thereby improving the expressiveness and retrievability of the knowledge base. Finally, the enhanced knowledge is embedded and organized through index construction, enabling multi-granularity hybrid retrieval.

During the online stage, user queries undergo a rewriting mechanism to improve clarity and maintain context continuity. Relevant knowledge is then retrieved via a retrieval and re-ranking process. Task-specific prompts are constructed from the top-ranked results, and answer generation and result presentation are performed by a large language model. This hierarchical pipeline enhances retrieval precision and answer quality across diverse intelligent question answering scenarios (see Fig. 1).

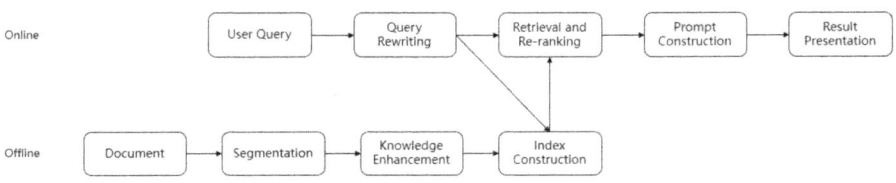

Fig. 1. RAG System Flowchart

Offline Processing Pipeline. The offline stage of the RAG system is responsible for transforming raw multimodal documents into structured and retrievable knowledge representations. It begins with a chunking module that integrates rule-based heuristics and large-model-driven semantic segmentation to partition documents into contextually coherent and semantically meaningful units. Such fine-grained segmentation enhances both the retrievability and interpretability of the knowledge.

Following segmentation, the knowledge enhancement module enriches the content through semantic augmentation. Leveraging multimodal large models, the system extracts and interprets embedded visual information—such as charts and figures—generating structured metadata including image type labels and descriptive captions. Concurrently, textual chunks are augmented with semantic summaries, keyword tags, and entity annotations. These enrichments increase the semantic density of the knowledge base, thereby improving retrieval granularity and recall accuracy.

The enriched content is subsequently processed by the index construction module, which builds a dual-retrieval structure: (1) high-dimensional dense embeddings are computed using pretrained encoders to support semantic search, and (2) sparse lexical indices are created via keyword-based systems such as ElasticSearch. This hybrid indexing strategy ensures robust coverage for both exact matching and semantically similar queries, forming a solid foundation for the subsequent online answering stage.

Online Question Answering Pipeline. The online stage focuses on delivering accurate and context-aware answers in real time. It commences with a query rewriting module that dynamically reformulates user questions by incorporating conversation history. This module leverages language model capabilities to clarify ambiguous expressions and standardize query formats, thereby enhancing retrieval alignment.

The rewritten query is then processed by the retrieval and re-ranking module, which searches the pre-built hybrid index. By combining sparse keyword retrieval with dense vector similarity, the system retrieves a candidate pool of relevant knowledge chunks. These candidates are ranked according to a scoring function that balances semantic relevance and information richness, ensuring that the top-k results are optimally suited for downstream generation.

Next, the prompt construction module integrates the original user query, the selected top-k knowledge chunks, and relevant conversational context to compose the input for the generative model. This composite prompt is fed into a large pretrained generative model, which synthesizes a fluent and factually grounded answer. The final response is then presented to the user in natural language, thus completing the intelligent question answering cycle.

System Evaluation Methodology. To rigorously assess the effectiveness of the RAG system in intelligent question answering tasks, we design a comprehensive multi-level automated evaluation framework. Retrieval performance is measured against real annotated datasets using standardized metrics such as precision and recall, which objectively quantify the accuracy of retrieved chunks relative to gold-standard answers.

For answer generation evaluation, a large language model is employed for end-to-end automated scoring. The original user query, retrieved chunks, generated answers, and reference answers are jointly input to the model, which automatically generates scores across multiple evaluation dimensions based on predefined criteria. This integrated evaluation framework substantially improves assessment efficiency and objectivity, providing robust support for continuous system optimization and scenario adaptability analysis.

3.2 Offline Phase

In intelligent question answering scenarios, the RAG system employs an offline processing pipeline to preprocess and enhance the original knowledge content, thereby establishing a robust data foundation for subsequent efficient and high-quality information retrieval and answer generation. The offline phase comprises several critical stages, including knowledge chunking, knowledge enhancement, knowledge structuring, and index construction. The choice of specific strategies at each stage directly impacts the ultimate performance and user experience of the question answering system. The following subsections provide a detailed comparison and analysis of the main processing strategies.

Chunking Strategies. Knowledge chunking represents the initial step in the offline pipeline, aiming to segment large-scale raw documents into semantically coherent and retrieval-friendly knowledge units. An appropriate chunking strategy balances information integrity and retrieval granularity, thereby enhancing the effectiveness and efficiency of subsequent question answering processes. The prevalent chunking strategies include:

Hierarchical Chunking. The hierarchical chunking approach combines rule-based methods with large language model (LLM) capabilities. Specifically, rule-based techniques such as regular expressions are employed to identify hierarchical headings and subheadings within document structures. Subsequently, large language models verify the semantic coherence and accuracy of these headers, enabling multilevel document segmentation. Following segmentation, dispersed but thematically related chunks are merged through aggregation mechanisms to form highly coherent knowledge units. This approach maximally preserves the original logical structure of the documents, ensures strong internal semantic cohesion within each chunk, and facilitates effective downstream retrieval and context-aware answer generation.

Recursive Character-Based Chunking. This strategy relies on predefined segmentation characters, such as periods, line breaks, or list markers—to iteratively segment long texts at multiple granularities. If the resulting chunk size or semantic coverage falls short of predefined thresholds, further recursive segmentation is applied using finer-grained delimiters. This ensures each chunk remains concise while maintaining semantic completeness.

Fixed-Length Character Chunking. The fixed-length character chunking method uses a fixed character count as the segmentation criterion, truncating content into chunks of predetermined size, typically aligned with the maximum token limits of downstream retrieval or generation models. Its simplicity and computational efficiency render it particularly suitable for preprocessing large-scale datasets.

Knowledge Enhancement. The knowledge enhancement stage focuses on expanding, enriching, and supplementing chunked knowledge units by leveraging external large models and multimodal understanding technologies, thereby improving retrieval accuracy and answer diversity in downstream question answering tasks. The major enhancement strategies include:

Question Generation Enhancement. Question generation enhancement methods autonomously generate sets of questions closely related to each knowledge chunk, establishing indexed mappings between these questions and their corresponding chunks. Utilizing advanced language modeling capabilities, key perspectives and potential user needs are extracted from each chunk to generate diverse and natural language questions. These generated questions enrich the retrieval entry points of the knowledge base and enable natural user queries to achieve high semantic recall of optimal chunks. Consequently, this approach significantly improves the naturalness of human-computer interaction and broadens query coverage, while effectively mitigating information loss caused by expression mismatches during retrieval.

Summarization Enhancement. Summarization enhancement aims to compress and abstract the content of each knowledge chunk. Large models generate high-quality textual summaries that are mapped to their respective chunks. During retrieval, user queries can be semantically matched against these summaries to facilitate recall of the most relevant original knowledge units. Summaries reduce redundant information and noise, thus improving retrieval efficiency and enabling rapid optimization in large-scale knowledge bases. Advances in summarization techniques ensure that the produced summaries balance comprehensive coverage with high abstraction, offering practical value for long-document comprehension and key information extraction.

Image Understanding. Image understanding strategies target multimodal content within original documents, enabling automated semantic parsing of visual data. Multimodal large models are leveraged to generate detailed category labels and textual descriptions for images, including tables, diagrams, blueprints, and various unstructured visual elements. A mapping is established between images and their corresponding textual descriptions, supporting retrieval of relevant images and associated content via text-based queries. This strategy enhances the system's ability to handle complex multimodal data and expands the channels through which visual information can be retrieved within question answering frameworks.

Knowledge Structuring. Effective knowledge structuring is essential for enhancing retrieval efficiency and improving the interpretability of large language models. The primary strategies employed include:

Integration of Titles and Categorical Tags. Documents are classified hierarchically across multiple levels, including domain, topic, and subtopic, with all titles preserved as explicit contextual labels for knowledge units. This structured classification facilitates precise content filtering during retrieval and supports downstream statistical analysis and visualization.

Integration of Structured Image Information. For documents containing domain-specific visual content—such as engineering blueprints or process flowcharts—structured tags and textual descriptions are generated to encode the images. Annotations may include node attributes, relational links, and other structural elements. These enrichments aid large models in complex scene reasoning and substantially augment the informational richness of the knowledge base.

Indexing Strategies. Offline indexing is a critical component to ensure efficient query processing within RAG systems. The main indexing methods encompass keyword-based and semantic retrieval techniques:

Keyword (Elasticsearch) Indexing. Utilizing technologies such as Elasticsearch, inverted indices are constructed over keywords, tags, generated questions, summaries, titles, and other relevant attributes of each knowledge chunk. This approach enables rapid retrieval responses while maintaining structural simplicity and interpretability.

Semantic Similarity (Embedding Model) Indexing. Advanced embedding models—such as BGE-M3 and the GME series—encode content from chunks, summaries, and generated questions into high-dimensional dense vectors. These vectors support efficient semantic retrieval via vector similarity search, effectively bridging semantic gaps induced by diverse user expressions. The composability of semantic embeddings further enables multi-stage recall and complex aggregation strategies. For multimodal data, semantic embeddings facilitate unified cross-modal retrieval.

Hybrid Indexing Strategy. By integrating keyword-based and semantic indexing, multiple complementary indices are constructed for the same knowledge content. Reranking models are subsequently employed to maximize recall accuracy and coverage. This hybrid approach offers strong adaptability, allowing dynamic adjustment of retrieval pathways based on query characteristics and striking an optimal balance between retrieval effectiveness and computational efficiency.

3.3   Online Pipeline

For intelligent question answering tasks, RAG systems typically adopt a multi-stage pipeline to achieve efficient and high-quality end-to-end question answering capabilities. The online module primarily focuses on four core stages: question rewriting, knowledge chunk retrieval, reranking, and answer generation.

Question Rewriting. In real-world applications, intelligent question answering systems frequently encounter multi-turn dialogues, where user queries are often closely tied to preceding conversational context. To mitigate semantic omissions and unclear references in multi-turn interactions, and to effectively improve the clarity and completeness of query expressions, this study employs a large language model (such as GPT-like models) for question rewriting. Specifically, the current dialogue history and the user's latest input are concatenated and fed into a large language model, generating a restated question enriched with complete contextual information. This strategy automatically supplements critical information, resolves omissions or references, and produces a new, contextually self-contained question text. The process can be formalized as the following conversion function:

$$Q' = \text{Rewriter}(C, Q)$$

where C denotes the entire preceding dialogue context, Q is the current user input, Rewriter refers to the large model-based rewriting module, and Q' represents the generated, context-consistent question.

Systematic question rewriting maximizes the expressive richness of the original question and provides an accurate semantic foundation for subsequent retrieval and content generation modules.

Knowledge Chunk Retrieval. Efficient retrieval of knowledge chunks is a key step to ensure answer accuracy in RAG systems. The retrieval stage aims to extract highly relevant text chunks (segments) from a large-scale knowledge base based on the rewritten question Q'. This study compares retrieval strategies and primarily utilizes two mainstream techniques: dense semantic matching with BGE-m3, and the classical inverted-index and keyword-based Elasticsearch (ES) system.

BGE-m3 is a vector retrieval model designed for multilingual and multi-task scenarios. It maps both queries and knowledge base chunks into a high-dimensional dense vector space, enabling high-quality semantic retrieval based on similarity metrics (such as inner product or cosine similarity). The process proceeds as follows:

- Encode the rewritten question Q' into a dense vector $\mathbf{h}_Q$;
- Pre-encode all chunks in the knowledge base to obtain vectors $\{\mathbf{h}_{c_i}\}$;
- Compute similarity scores between $\mathbf{h}_Q$ and $\mathbf{h}_{c_i}$, and select the top-k chunks with the highest scores as retrieval results.

$$\text{Recall Top-k}(Q', \mathcal{C}) = \underset{c_i \in \mathcal{C}}{\text{top-}k}\ \text{sim}(\mathbf{h}_Q, \mathbf{h}_{c_i}) \tag{1}$$

Here, $\mathcal{C}$ denotes the set of knowledge base chunks, and $\text{sim}(\cdot, \cdot)$ represents the vector similarity function.

Elasticsearch (ES), based on inverted index and utilizing BM25 for retrieval, is also adopted. Based on the performance of retrieval relevance, this system systematically compares the effectiveness of the aforementioned approaches.

Reranking. The top-k chunks obtained during retrieval may still contain irrelevant content. To further enhance the relevance and effectiveness of the generated answers, a large-scale pretrained reranking model, bge-reranker-v2-m3, is introduced for optimization of candidate chunk ordering. The bge-reranker-v2-m3 model offers robust fine-grained cross-chunk semantic modeling, enabling assessment of each chunk's contextual completeness and degree of match with Q'.

The reranking process is as follows:

- For each chunk c_i in the candidate set, input both Q' and c_i into the bge-reranker-v2-m3 model to obtain a relevance score s_i;
- Rank all chunks in descending order according to s_i;
- Select the top-k' chunks with the highest scores for answer generation.

$$\text{Rerank}(Q', \{c_1, ..., c_k\}) = \text{top-}k'\ \text{by}\ s_i = \text{Reranker}(Q', c_i) \tag{2}$$

This reranking strategy significantly reduces semantic noise introduced during preliminary retrieval, ensuring that the text fragments supporting answer generation are maximally semantically aligned with the actual question.

Answer Generation. Answer generation is the final stage in the RAG system and has a direct impact on the overall question answering experience. In this stage, the question Q' and the top-k' relevant chunks selected after reranking are concatenated into a final prompt and fed into a large pretrained language model (such as a Transformer-based generative model) to generate natural language answers.

Specifically:

- Organize the input template by concatenating the question with the content of the top-k' chunks to form the conditional context;
- Input into the large language model for inference to generate a fluent, informative, and highly referential answer text A;
- Output the result as the final user response.

$$A = \text{LLM-Generate}(Q', \text{Concat}(c_{i_1}, ..., c_{i_{k'}})) \qquad (3)$$

This strategy not only ensures semantic accuracy, but also improves information fusion capabilities and content coverage, thereby significantly enhancing the overall question answering performance.

Collaboration Mechanism Among Modules. To ensure efficient collaboration across all stages, the system design thoroughly optimizes input-output coupling. The output of question rewriting offers semantically robust new questions, facilitating downstream knowledge retrieval. The retrieval module outputs a rich candidate set, reserving maximal potentially effective information for reranking. The reranking strategy guarantees high-quality, relevant fragments for the generation model. Each module mutually enhances the others, forming an efficient end-to-end RAG question answering pipeline.

3.4   Evaluation

This study establishes a rigorous and comprehensive multidimensional automated evaluation framework to quantitatively assess system performance from both retrieval and generation perspectives.

Retrieval Effectiveness Evaluation. An automated evaluation method is employed to measure the recall accuracy of the retrieval module. The core metric used is top-k accuracy, which determines whether the ground-truth answer fragments are present within the top-k retrieved results. Specifically, for each query, if the standard answer chunk appears among the top-k retrieved candidates, it is considered a hit. By varying k, this metric comprehensively evaluates the retrieval module's ability to capture relevant information, thereby providing an objective quantitative basis for subsequent answer generation stages.

Summarization Effectiveness Evaluation. For the evaluation of the generation module, large-scale language models are leveraged to conduct end-to-end automated scoring. Each question answering instance comprises the original query, the retrieved knowledge chunks, the model-generated answer, and the corresponding human reference answer, all integrated as the evaluation context. During assessment, the large language model applies a set of predefined multidimensional criteria—including relevance, factual correctness, completeness, logical coherence, and structural organization—to assign scores for each aspect of the generated response. The weighting and definitions of these criteria conform to established standards in the intelligent question answering research community. The automated scoring results serve as a reliable reference for comparative analyses across different RAG system configurations, effectively reflecting their overall performance in real-world QA scenarios.

This comprehensive evaluation framework enables multidimensional, end-to-end quantitative comparisons of RAG systems in intelligent question answering, thereby providing a solid theoretical foundation and empirical support for continuous system improvement and optimization.

4 Experimental Analysis

4.1 Experimental Setup

This study systematically evaluates a range of retrieval-augmented strategies for a customized multimodal RAG question answering task. Elasticsearch (ES) serves as the baseline keyword retrieval method, while vector retrieval models including BGE-M3 and the multimodal-capable GME model (2 billion parameters) are employed to benchmark improvements in terms of top-k hit rate—the proportion of retrieved results containing the correct answer. Several text enhancement techniques are implemented, including label enhancement (utilizing title and category metadata), structural enhancement (e.g., incorporation of structured table representations), question enhancement, and summary enhancement. Furthermore, advanced retrieval strategies such as hybrid retrieval and multi-stage retrieval are explored to assess their impact on overall system performance.

4.2 Experimental Results and Analysis

Retrieval Effectiveness Analysis. Table 1 presents detailed hit rates for various retrieval strategies and enhancement configurations. The comparative results demonstrate that, within the original document retrieval setting (top-5), the BGE and GME models achieve hit rates of 64.15% and 75.47%, respectively—significantly outperforming the ES baseline at 45.28%. As the top-k threshold increases, all models exhibit further gains in retrieval hit rates, with the GME model reaching a maximum hit rate of 86.79% at top-10.

Further analysis of various information enhancement strategies shows that under the label enhancement scenario (e.g., TitleCategory_Enhanced), the BGE and GME models reach hit rates of 83.02% and 90.57% (top-10). The introduction of structural information (StructureBlueprint_Enhanced and FullStructure_Enhanced) also brings consistent gains, providing several additional percentage points of improvement. For summary enhancement and question enhancement, the increments are more moderate but still outperform the baseline, underscoring the importance of information aggregation and focus. Generally, hybrid retrieval—combining keyword and vector-based retrieval—fully exploits the respective strengths. Under GME hybrid retrieval at top-9 and top-10 settings, the highest global hit rate is achieved (90.57%).

Analysis of Summary Response Performance. As shown in Table 1, the RAG system achieved outstanding results across all evaluation metrics in this intelligent question answering experiment. The overall score attainment rate

Table 1. Retrieval Effectiveness (%) for Different Enhancement Methods and Retrieval Strategies

Enhancement Method	top k	ES	BGE	BGE+ES	GME	GME+ES
Raw_Document	5	45.28%	64.15%	67.92%	75.47%	75.47%
Raw_Document	6	47.17%	67.92%	71.70%	77.36%	79.25%
Raw_Document	7	49.06%	71.70%	77.36%	77.36%	83.02%
Raw_Document	8	49.06%	73.58%	79.25%	83.02%	86.79%
Raw_Document	9	50.94%	73.58%	79.25%	84.91%	86.79%
Raw_Document	10	50.94%	77.36%	81.13%	86.79%	86.79%
TitleCategory_Enhanced	5	54.72%	79.25%	83.02%	81.13%	83.02%
TitleCategory_Enhanced	6	58.49%	81.13%	84.91%	81.13%	84.91%
TitleCategory_Enhanced	7	58.49%	81.13%	84.91%	84.91%	86.79%
TitleCategory_Enhanced	8	58.49%	81.13%	84.91%	86.79%	88.68%
TitleCategory_Enhanced	9	66.04%	81.13%	88.68%	90.57%	90.57%
TitleCategory_Enhanced	10	66.04%	83.02%	90.57%	90.57%	90.57%
StructureBlueprint_Enhanced	5	45.28%	64.15%	67.92%	73.58%	73.58%
StructureBlueprint_Enhanced	6	45.28%	67.92%	69.81%	75.47%	75.47%
StructureBlueprint_Enhanced	7	49.06%	71.70%	75.47%	75.47%	79.25%
StructureBlueprint_Enhanced	8	50.94%	73.58%	79.25%	81.13%	84.91%
StructureBlueprint_Enhanced	9	50.94%	73.58%	79.25%	83.02%	84.91%
StructureBlueprint_Enhanced	10	50.94%	77.36%	81.13%	84.91%	86.79%
FullStructure_Enhanced	5	54.72%	79.25%	83.02%	79.25%	81.13%
FullStructure_Enhanced	6	56.60%	79.25%	83.02%	79.25%	83.02%
FullStructure_Enhanced	7	60.38%	81.13%	84.91%	83.02%	86.79%
FullStructure_Enhanced	8	60.38%	81.13%	84.91%	84.91%	88.68%
FullStructure_Enhanced	9	66.04%	81.13%	88.68%	88.68%	90.57%
FullStructure_Enhanced	10	66.04%	83.02%	90.57%	88.68%	90.57%
Question_Enhanced	5	28.30%	60.38%	66.04%	56.60%	60.38%
Question_Enhanced	6	35.85%	60.38%	66.04%	60.38%	60.38%
Question_Enhanced	7	35.85%	60.38%	66.04%	64.15%	62.26%
Question_Enhanced	8	35.85%	60.38%	66.04%	66.04%	66.04%
Question_Enhanced	9	35.85%	62.26%	66.04%	66.04%	66.04%
Question_Enhanced	10	37.74%	62.26%	67.92%	66.04%	67.92%
Summary_Enhanced	5	52.83%	62.26%	69.81%	75.47%	77.36%
Summary_Enhanced	6	54.72%	64.15%	73.58%	77.36%	75.47%
Summary_Enhanced	7	54.72%	66.04%	75.47%	79.25%	77.36%
Summary_Enhanced	8	56.60%	66.04%	75.47%	81.13%	79.25%
Summary_Enhanced	9	56.60%	67.92%	77.36%	81.13%	79.25%
Summary_Enhanced	10	56.60%	67.92%	77.36%	81.13%	79.25%

reached 88.57%, indicating that the general response quality has reached an exceptionally high standard. Regarding relevance, 94.20% of samples received the highest possible score (1 point), demonstrating that the system effectively comprehends the underlying context and information needs behind user queries. The generated responses closely align with the input questions, providing direct and precise feedback that significantly enhances user experience.

Fact accuracy, a core dimension ensuring information credibility, achieved a high proportion of top scores (2 points) at 95.71%. In most cases, explicit evidence supporting the answers could be traced back to the original knowledge base, effectively mitigating issues such as hallucination. Only 1.43% of samples contained factual inaccuracies. This solidly underpins the usability and reliability of the intelligent question answering system.

Evaluation of answer structure and expression coherence revealed that 100% of samples attained full marks on both criteria. This indicates that the generative module of the RAG system possesses strong capabilities in natural language organization and logical articulation. The outputs comprehensively cover key information while ensuring seamless content flow and semantic fluency, thereby delivering responses that are clear and easily understood.

Particularly noteworthy is the indicator of structural clarity, for which all generated responses received the highest rating. This further validates that the adopted retrieval and generation strategies fully exploit the architectural advantages of the RAG framework, effectively avoiding common generative issues such as sentence disorder or incoherent structure. Moreover, the system demonstrates robust generalization and adaptability in complex scenarios, including automatic summarization and multi-turn dialogue. It efficiently integrates heterogeneous multi-source information and organizes output in a logically clear, well-structured, and hierarchical manner, substantially enhancing the practical value of the RAG model within intelligent question answering applications (Table 2).

Table 2. Evaluation metrics, score values, and their corresponding proportions.

Evaluation Metric	Score Value	Proportion (%)
Full Score	7	88.57
Relevance Score	1	94.2029
	0	5.7971
Factual Accuracy Score	2	95.7143
	1	2.8571
	0	1.4286
Completeness Score	2	100
Coherence Score	1	100
Structural Clarity Score	1	100

We evaluated the performance of various retrieval strategies on a custom multimodal retrieval generation task. The experiment showed significant improvements in retrieval hit rates when using label-enhanced, structured-enhanced, hybrid retrieval, and multi-stage retrieval strategies. The results indicated that hybrid retrieval strategies and structured data enhancement were critical in improving the retrieval performance.

5 Conclusion

This study systematically investigates and implements a multimodal retrieval-augmented generation (RAG) system tailored for intelligent question answering scenarios. Addressing key technical challenges in multi-source heterogeneous data comprehension, semantic alignment, efficient retrieval, and automatic generation within complex knowledge environments, we propose a series of innovative hierarchical solutions. The methodology integrates fine-grained offline knowledge segmentation and multidimensional enhancement techniques with automated comprehension and structured annotation via multimodal large models, thereby achieving high-quality knowledge representation and comprehensive indexing of content and context.

In the online phase, the system incorporates multi-turn dialogue rewriting, efficient hybrid retrieval, refined re-ranking, and large model-based generation to construct an end-to-end closed-loop question answering pipeline. For evaluation, we develop a multidimensional automated framework that quantitatively assesses system performance across various facets, including retrieval accuracy, factual consistency, generation quality, and structural clarity.

Experimental results demonstrate that the proposed RAG system significantly improves retrieval hit rates under diverse enhancement and hybrid retrieval strategies, effectively overcoming limitations of individual models in handling multimodal and complex structured knowledge. The generated answers attain high standards of relevance, factual accuracy, logical coherence, and structural organization, evidencing robust capabilities in information fusion and knowledge integration.

This work not only advances the technical foundations of intelligent question answering systems but also validates the effective synergy among multimodal processing, large-scale language models, and RAG architectures. Furthermore, it establishes a solid theoretical and engineering basis for deploying such systems at scale in demanding domains such as healthcare, finance, and education.

Acknowledgments. This work is supported by National Key Research and Development Project, No. 2023YFB3308502.

Disclosure of Interests. The authors declare that they have no known competing financial interests or personal relationships that could have appeared to influence the work reported in this paper.

References

1. Yu, H., Yu, C., Wang, Z., Zou, D., Qin, H.: Enhancing healthcare through large language models: a study on medical question answering. In: 2024 IEEE 6th International Conference on Power, Intelligent Computing and Systems (ICPICS), pp. 895–900. IEEE (2024)
2. Sajja, R., Sermet, Y., Cikmaz, M., Cwiertny, D., Demir, I.: Artificial intelligence-enabled intelligent assistant for personalized and adaptive learning in higher education. Information **15**(10), 596 (2024)
3. Li, Y., Wang, S., Ding, H., et al.: Large language models in finance: a survey. In: Proceedings of the Fourth ACM International Conference on AI in Finance, pp. 374–382 (2023)
4. Liu, B., He, L., Liu, Y., Yu, T., Xiang, Y., Zhu, L., Ruan, W.: Transformer-based multimodal infusion dialogue systems. Electronics **11**(20), 3409 (2022)
5. Lewis, P., et al.: Retrieval-augmented generation for knowledge-intensive NLP tasks. Adv. Neural. Inf. Process. Syst. **33**, 9459–9474 (2020)
6. Amazon Web Services. What is rag? Retrieval-augmented generation ai explained. https://aws.amazon.com/what-is/retrieval-augmented-generation/ (2024). Accessed 17 May 2025
7. NVIDIA Technical Blog. Lost in the middle: improving llms' long-context retrieval using rag with nvidia nemo. https://developer.nvidia.com/blog/improving-llm-long-context-retrieval-using-rag-with-nvidia-nemo/ (2023). Accessed 17 May 2025
8. Liu, N.F., et al.: Lost in the middle: how language models use long contexts. arXiv preprint arXiv:2307.03172 (2023)
9. Trappolini, G., Santilli, A., Rodolà, E., Halevy, A., Silvestri, F.: Multimodal neural databases. In: Proceedings of the 46th International ACM SIGIR Conference on Research and Development in Information Retrieval, pp. 2619–2628 (2023)
10. Liu, B., Song, R., Xiang, Y., Du, J., Ruan, W., Hu, J.: Self-supervised entity alignment based on multi-modal contrastive learning. IEEE/CAA J. Autom. Sinica **9**(11), 2031–2033 (2022)
11. Robertson, S., Zaragoza, H., et al.: The probabilistic relevance framework: Bm25 and beyond. Found. Trends Inf. Retr. **3**(4), 333–389 (2009)
12. Chen, J., et al.: BGE m3-embedding: multi-lingual, multi-functionality, multi-granularity text embeddings through self-knowledge distillation. arXiv preprint arXiv:2402.03216 (2024)
13. Zhang, X., et al.: GME: improving universal multimodal retrieval by multimodal LLMs. arXiv preprint arXiv:2412.16855 (2024)
14. Achiam, J., et al.: GPT-4 technical report. arXiv preprint arXiv:2303.08774 (2023)
15. Bai, J., et al.: Qwen-VL: a frontier large vision-language model with versatile abilities. arXiv preprint arXiv:2308.12966 (2023)
16. Yang, A., et al.: Qwen2 technical report. arXiv preprint arXiv:2407.10671 (2024)
17. Qwen Team. Qwen2.5: a party of foundation models. https://qwenlm.github.io/blog/qwen2.5/ (2024)
18. Mialon, G., et al.: Augmented language models: a survey. arXiv preprint arXiv:2302.07842 (2023)
19. Li, C., Liu, Z., Xiao, S., Shao, Y.: Making large language models a better foundation for dense retrieval. arXiv preprint arXiv:2312.15503 (2023)

From Determinism to Probabilism: Reshaping the Causation Identification of Medical Malpractice in AI-Assisted Diagnosis and Treatment

Wen Wang[1], Ang Yang[2]📧, Zhao Li[2]📧, and Yunbo Gong[3](✉)📧

[1] College of Modern Economics and Management JXUFE, Nanchang 330013, China
[2] Law School, Jiangxi University of Finance and Economics, Nanchang 330013, China
[3] Law School, Xi'an Jiaotong University, Xi'an 710049, China
yunbo.gong@outlook.com

Abstract. The integration of artificial intelligence (AI) assisted diagnosis and treatment has ushered in a new era of healthcare, but it also presents significant challenges to traditional theories of causation in medical malpractice liability. This paper examines the limitations of conventional causation determination methods in the context of AI-assisted diagnosis and proposes a shift toward probabilistic causation theory. We construct a rule system centered on "probability gain" supported by apparent cause identification, joint causation identification, spurious cause analysis, and causal chain reconstruction. This approach assists courts in determining causation when evidentiary proof is limited and causation is uncertain. We demonstrate how this framework can clarify the roles of medical personnel and AI entities in mixed causation cases and determine the attributable causal power and liability share in joint causation scenarios. Our findings suggest that probabilistic causation theory offers a promising avenue for unraveling the complex causation puzzles in AI-assisted medical malpractice cases, potentially reshaping the legal landscape for healthcare liability in the age of artificial intelligence.

Keywords: Artificial intelligence assisted diagnosis and treatment · Medical malpractice liability · Proof of causality · Probabilistic causality

1 Introduction

Artificial intelligence technology is reshaping medical practice, with diagnostic and therapeutic AI systems providing crucial decision support to healthcare professionals [1]. These systems demonstrate significant potential in medical imaging interpretation, personalized treatment planning, and risk prediction such as hypoxemia prevention [2], marking a new era of intelligent medical practice.

© The Author(s), under exclusive license to Springer Nature Switzerland AG 2026
Y. Yang et al. (Eds.): ICCC 2025, LNCS 16156, pp. 20–35, 2026.
https://doi.org/10.1007/978-3-032-06310-6_2

However, the rapid advancement of diagnostic AI presents unprecedented challenges to legal frameworks, particularly in medical malpractice liability causation determination. The probabilistic complexity, opacity, dynamic optimization, and decision-making autonomy of AI algorithms make causation proof exceptionally difficult in malpractice cases [3]. Traditional causation theories including the "but for" rule, proximate cause doctrine, foreseeability standard, and substantial factor test—struggle to delineate responsibilities in human-machine collaborative environments.

This challenge reflects fundamental limitations in existing legal frameworks. Causation determination in AI-assisted medical practice has evolved from simple linear inference to complex multi-factor networks, challenging legal practitioners and legislators alike. Inadequate resolution may stifle medical innovation and encourage conservative technology adoption. Therefore, developing AI-era causation paradigms has become crucial for the legal community. This article proposes a "probability gain"-centered causation determination model [4] to address these pressing issues.

Traditional causation theories reveal significant limitations when applied to diagnostic AI challenges. Understanding these limitations is essential for developing effective liability frameworks for AI-assisted medical malpractice cases.

1.1 Traditional Causation Theories in Medical Malpractice

Despite promising prospects, diagnostic AI presents significant risks. Misdiagnoses can cause severe consequences, including unnecessary medical expenses from algorithmic errors [5]. Unlike traditional medical devices [6], AI decision-making processes are difficult to assess intuitively, necessitating causation establishment for producer accountability [7]. Traditional medical malpractice causation determination employs four primary methods: the "but-for" test, proximate cause principle, foreseeability standard, and substantial factor test.

The but-for test, derived from conditio sine qua non theory, establishes causation when damage would not occur absent the specific action. In Yu Enhui v. Chongqing Southwest Hospital, the court found that while the patient's death primarily resulted from pre-existing conditions, the hospital's wrongful actions were necessary causal factors [8]. However, this proves overly mechanical for complex medical cases. The proximate cause principle identifies legally responsible direct causes among multiple factual causes, requiring immediate connection between action and damage. If A injures B, but B dies in a hospital-route car accident, only the accident constitutes the legal cause of death. While limiting liability scope, judgment standards remain subjective.

The foreseeability standard assesses actors' reasonable ability to anticipate causal chains between conduct and consequences [9]. Courts incorporate professional backgrounds when evaluating understanding of potential causal relationships. For surgical complications, courts consider whether reasonable surgeons could foresee that chosen methods might interact with patient conditions to cause harm.

The substantial factor test balances the "but-for" test's broad scope with proximate cause limitations, recognizing only conditions typically sufficient to cause specific harm based on empirical rules [10]. In Bolitho v. City and Hackney Health Authority [11], the House of Lords considered not only delayed arrival but whether timely arrival would have led to intubation conforming to responsible medical practice standards.

1.2   The Challenges of Diagnostic AI to Traditional Theories of Causation

Diagnostic AI revolutionizes medical practice while posing unprecedented challenges to traditional causation theories. These challenges manifest in four aspects:

The Failure of the "but-For" Rule in Cases of Probabilistic Complexity. Diagnostic AI presents dual challenges to the "but-for" rule: multiple-cause complexity and probabilistic decision-making. Patient health outcomes now result from multiple interacting factors—physician judgment, AI recommendations, training data quality, and individual patient differences [12]—rather than single medical decisions. This complex causal network challenges the "but-for" rule's fundamental assumption that single factors have determinative impact. Each factor's influence may be partial, conditional, or interdependent, making isolated factor consideration nearly impossible [13]. Traditional counterfactual reasoning methods inadequately reflect true causal relationships, potentially causing factor influence misestimation.

The probabilistic decision-making mechanism fundamentally challenges the deterministic causal concept underlying the "but-for" rule. AI diagnostic recommendations, based on complex statistical models, are inherently probabilistic and may produce different outputs with identical inputs [14]. This challenges traditional causal reasoning's assumption that single decisive factors can be clearly identified and removed. AI systems alter the entire decision-making process's probability distribution rather than single decisive factors [15]. AI recommendations typically influence physicians' overall decision inclinations rather than causing or preventing specific decisions [16]. This complex probabilistic interaction renders traditional counterfactual reasoning ("but for X, Y would not have occurred") difficult to apply.

The Dilemma of Inexplicability and the Proximate Cause Principle. The inexplicability of diagnostic AI poses a fundamental challenge to the application of the proximate cause principle. The proximate cause principle requires courts to identify the most direct and immediate cause in a complex causal chain. However, the "black box" nature of AI systems makes this task nearly impossible [17]. In traditional medical cases, courts can trace the proximate cause of harm by examining the doctor's diagnostic process and medication decisions. In cases involving AI, even if the input data and final output are observable, the intermediate decision-making process is often opaque. For instance, in a medical imaging diagnostic system that employs deep learning, knowing that the system classified an X-ray as showing a tumor does not easily reveal which features of the image and what inferential paths led to this judgment [18].

This inexplicability challenges the fundamental assumption of proximate cause theory, which posits the ability to identify a decisive turning point in the causal chain. In AI systems, decisions are based on the principle of "distributed representation," where information is not stored in a specific location but dispersed across the network's weights [19]. Each decision results from the interaction of thousands of parameters within the network, making it difficult to view any single parameter as the decisive factor. For example, in a diagnostic AI system, even if the activation of a specific neuron significantly influences the final diagnosis, this neuron cannot be equated with the proximate cause. This is because the activation of this neuron is influenced by numerous inputs from preceding layers of neurons, forming an intricate causal network [20]. Such complex internal interdependencies make it challenging to isolate a single, decisive factor that can be considered the proximate cause, fundamentally challenging the applicability of the proximate cause principle.

Dynamic Optimization and the Ambiguity of the Foreseeability Standard. AI systems' dynamic learning capabilities pose unprecedented challenges to traditional foreseeability standards. Autonomous learning allows systems to continually optimize performance, demonstrating capabilities beyond initial design intentions. However, this evolving nature causes system behavior to deviate from designers' original intent, resulting in unforeseeable outcomes. The learning process involves multi-layered, multi-dimensional information integration and reconstruction through complex neural networks rather than simple linear accumulation. While deep learning creativity holds significant potential for improving diagnostic efficiency, it renders decision-making pathways difficult to trace and predict, challenging causation proof.

Dynamic optimization processes may introduce or amplify errors. Without trusted data circulation systems, data quality issues severely threaten AI system reliability. Diagnostic AI systems may significantly alter decision logic through continuous learning and self-adjustment within short periods. This process involves parameter fine-tuning, autonomous algorithmic architecture restructuring, and multi-system co-evolution. Such complex dynamic optimization mechanisms make system behavior highly uncertain, exceeding traditional foreseeability standard scope. Dynamic optimization may produce "emergent behaviors," where systems exhibit entirely unforeseen functions or behavior patterns. This unpredictability and behavioral emergence fundamentally undermine traditional foreseeability standard applicability.

The Misalignment Between Decision Autonomy and the Theory of Proximate Cause. AI systems' autonomous decision-making fundamentally challenges proximate cause theory, disrupting traditional legal causation frameworks. Conventional theory asserts that only actions generally sufficient to cause specific harm according to empirical rules constitute legal causes. However, AI systems' extraordinary pattern recognition and data analysis capabilities circumvent this constraint. In medical imaging, AI demonstrates exceptional proficiency detecting subtle features eluding human physicians, such as identifying minute lung cancer lesions overlooked during routine examinations [21]. This capability transcends human cognitive boundaries, challenging traditional understanding of "generally sufficient to cause a result" while blurring the lines between empirical medicine and system diagnostics.

More problematic are intelligent systems' multi-layered, non-linear causal networks, which further undermine proximate cause theory foundations. Unlike traceable human physician diagnostic processes, system decisions may involve complex interactions among millions of parameters. When predicting patient prognosis, systems integrate multidimensional data—genetic information, lifestyle, medical history, and current symptoms—weaving intricate decision-making webs. Equating any single factor to a cause "generally sufficient to produce the result" becomes impossible. This complexity renders causal chains elusive and challenges courts' traditional understanding of "proximate." The legal community must reconsider: What causation in system decision-making networks can be deemed proximate? How can proximate causation be identified and evaluated within these digital complexities [22]?

Diagnostic AI poses comprehensive challenges to traditional causation theories. From "but-for" rule failures to proximate cause tracing dilemmas, foreseeability standard ambiguity, and proximate cause theory misalignment, AI systems' inherent complexity, opacity, dynamic optimization, and autonomous decision-making have profoundly transformed medical malpractice liability determination contexts. These challenges highlight traditional causation theories' limitations facing new technologies and underscore urgent needs for developing AI-era compatible causation frameworks.

2   Methods

The technical characteristics of AI systems and their auxiliary role in diagnostic and treatment scenarios, while exacerbating the uncertainty of causation, do not negate the existence of causation. The main reason for the difficulty in proving causation in judicial practice is the excessively high standard of proof. Acceptance of such a high standard of proof is a consequence of people's belief in causal determinism. Throughout the development of modern science and philosophy, determinism has been highly controversial. Probability has become an important factor in understanding the laws of the world and in judging causation. Although accepting a probabilistic causation does not suffice to overturn determinism [23], it can reduce the difficulty of proving causation in the context of establishing liability for medical harm caused by diagnostic AI.

2.1 Paradigm Shift in Causation Toward Probabilistic Thinking

Determinism has persisted as causation theory's central thread, embodying necessity, universality, and predictability principles. Originating from Aristotle's four causes doctrine and refined during the scientific revolution, determinism depicts the universe as a precisely operating machine where every event is determined by preceding causes. Newtonian mechanics reinforced deterministic causation, viewing natural laws as immutable principles governing all phenomena. Determinism permeates legal practice, manifested in the "but-for" rule requiring necessary connections between conduct and outcome. However, this stringent perspective reveals limitations when confronting complex realities. Hume noted that causation constancy might be human mind illusion [24]. Kant's attempt to defend causation necessity through priori reasoning failed to resolve this dilemma [25], laying groundwork for probabilistic causation theories.

Modern scientific theories, particularly quantum mechanics, fundamentally shook determinism's foundation, driving causal theory toward more inclusive paradigms. Max Born declared quantum law discovery marked strict determinism's end [26], while Heisenberg asserted causality's inherently probabilistic nature [27]. Quantum mechanics' core principles—uncertainty principle and probabilistic wave function interpretation-profoundly challenge traditional causality notions [28]. This scientific revolution transformed understanding from simple, linear, deterministic relationships to complex, probabilistic correlations. Against this paradigm shift, probabilistic causality theory emerged, offering new causal relationship frameworks. Patrick Suppes argued that since fully grasping all outcome-influencing factors is often impossible, causal relationships must be described probabilistically [29]. This aligns with Hume's earlier probabilistic causality notion. Probabilistic causality theory's basic premise treats causal relationships as probabilistic dependencies rather than deterministic certainties. Scholars developed several approaches: conditional probability (Suppes and Reichenbach), interventionist approaches (Pearl [30]), and Bayesian networks [31].

Probabilistic thinking evolution reshaped philosophy of science and permeated legal practice. Legal fields embraced probabilistic reasoning naturally. In toxic tort cases, courts' acceptance of statistical epidemiological evidence acknowledges causation's probabilistic nature [32]. With emerging technologies like AI, probabilistic thinking's importance in legal causality determination becomes evident. The EU Expert Group on Liability and New Technologies [33] explicitly advocates shifting from deterministic to probabilistic approaches for AI-related cases.

Probabilistic causality theory offers paradigm shifts in legal reasoning, fundamentally challenging traditional deterministic legal causation paradigms. Deterministic perspectives view causation as necessary and certain, with event connection probability fixed at 1. Probabilistic causality theory reinterprets causal relationships as probabilistic dependencies, where probability P ranges from 0 to 1, breaking rigid binary causation definitions and infusing analysis with flexibility.

When applying probabilistic causality theory judicially, selecting appropriate theoretical approaches is crucial. The conditional probability approach, due to intuitiveness and practicality, integrates more easily with traditional legal reasoning, quantifying causal relationship strength while capturing uncertainty and complexity. The interventionist approach faces courtroom intervention scenario replication challenges, while Bayesian networks require extensive data and intricate computations creating gaps with current judicial practice demands. Probabilistic reasoning application in legal proof requires nuanced understanding of direct and indirect probabilistic inferences. Prakken distinguishes direct probabilistic reasoning (drawing conclusions from statistical evidence) from indirect probabilistic reasoning (using probabilities to assess argument strength within inferential structures) [34]. This distinction becomes crucial for AI-assisted medical decision-making's multi-layered causal networks.

We propose a causality determination framework comprising four core rules: apparent cause identification, joint causality determination, spurious cause distinction, and screening-off causal chain reconstruction.

2.2 Theoretical Construction of Probabilistic Causality: a Revolution in the Legal Rules of Causation Determination

From this groundbreaking perspective, a causality determination framework can be constructed, comprising four core rules: the foundational rule for identifying apparent causes, the advanced rule for determining joint causality, the nuanced rule for distinguishing spurious causes, and the screening-off rule for reconstructing causal chains:

The Foundational Rule for Identifying Apparent Causes. Within probabilistic causality theory, apparent cause identification holds central position, assessing causality based on event occurrence probability. Let $P(A_t)$ represent event A's probability at time t, and $P(B_{t'})$ denote event B's probability at earlier time t'. $P(A_t|B_{t'})$ represents event A's probability at time t given event B occurred at time t'. According to Suppes, event B at time t' constitutes an apparent cause of event A at time t if the following conditions are met [35]: (1) $t' < t$; (2) $P(B_{t'}) > 0$; (3) $P(A_t|B_{t'}) > P(A_t)$. Event B at time t' does not necessarily cause event A at time t, but increases A's occurrence probability. Therefore, absent other interfering events disrupting the probabilistic connection between $P(B_{t'})$ and $P(A_t)$ [36], $P(B_{t'})$ can be considered an apparent cause of $P(A_t)$.

The Advanced Rule for Identifying Joint Causality. In complex causal networks, single apparent causes often cannot fully account for outcome events. Probabilistic causality theory developed joint causality identification methods, focusing on how multiple cause events collectively influence outcome event probability. Suppose event A is the outcome event, and events B and C are potential cause events, with $t'' < t' < t$. Joint causality identification requires the following conditions: (1) $P(B_{t''}) > 0$ and $P(C_{t'}) > 0$; (2) $P(A_t|B_{t''} \wedge C_{t'}) > P(A_t|B_{t''})$; (3) $P(A_t|B_{t''} \wedge C_{t'}) > P(A_t|C_{t'})$; (4) $P(A_t|B_{t''} \wedge C_{t'}) > P(A_t)$. Here, $P(A_t|B_{t''} \wedge C_{t'})$ represents event A's probability at time t given events B and C occur at times t'' and t', respectively [37]. These conditions reveal joint causality's essential characteristics. Condition (1) ensures cause events' actual occurrence possibility. Conditions (2) and (3) indicate combined effects exceed individual event impacts. Condition (4) guarantees joint causes increase overall outcome probability. Joint causality does not imply simple additive relationships between cause events. Complex interactions may exist, including synergistic effects where $P(A_t|B_{t''} \wedge C_{t'}) > P(A_t|B_{t''}) + P(A_t|C_{t'}) - P(A_t)$, indicating combined effects exceed individual effect sums [38]. Joint causality identification provides comprehensive perspectives for analyzing complex system causal relationships, particularly important in diagnostic AI where outcomes result from multiple factors. However, increasing factor numbers complicates causality identification, requiring cautious practical application.

The Nuanced Rule for Distinguishing Spurious Causes. Probabilistic causality theory not only identifies apparent causes and joint causality but also provides rules for distinguishing spurious causes within intermediate steps. These rules refine probabilistic relationship analysis, building on time series assumptions. Assume $t'' < t' < t$, where $C_{t''}$ denotes event C's probability at time t''. $P(A_t|C_{t''})$ represents event A's conditional probability at time t given event C occurred at time t''. $P(A_t|B_{t'} \wedge C_{t''})$ represents event A's conditional probability at time t given event C occurred at time t'', followed by event B at time t'. According to this theory, $B_{t'}$ can be identified as a spurious cause of A_t if the following conditions are satisfied: (1) $P(B_{t'} \wedge C_{t''}) > 0$; (2) $P(A_t|B_{t'} \wedge C_{t''}) = P(A_t|C_{t''})$; (3) $P(A_t|B_{t'} \wedge C_{t''}) \geq P(A_t|B_{t'})$. Condition (1) ensures events B and C's joint occurrence possibility, establishing analysis groundwork. Condition (2) reveals key characteristics: although $B_{t'}$ might independently cause A_t, earlier event $C_{t''}$ has already independently caused A_t with probability $P(A_t|C_{t''})$, and $B_{t'}$'s sequential occurrence following $C_{t''}$ does not increase this probability. Condition (3) excludes the possibility that $B_{t'}$ alone has higher probability of causing A_t than combined $B_{t'}$ and $C_{t''}$ occurrence. When these conditions are met, earlier event $C_{t''}$ screens off later event $B_{t'}$, effectively excluding $B_{t'}$ from the causal chain.

The Screening-Off Rule for Reconstructing Causal Chains. German philosopher Hans Reichenbach made significant contributions to probabilistic causality theory, notably his "screening-off rule" [39]. This rule elegantly addresses mediating effects within complex causal networks, providing powerful tools for understanding multiple causal relationships. The screening-off rule's core determines whether intermediary events can block causal connections between earlier events and final outcomes. It considers three temporally sequential events: $C_{t''}$, $B_{t'}$, and A_t. To establish screening-off effects, both $C_{t''}$ and $B_{t'}$ must be apparent causes of A_t, satisfying: $P(A_t|B_{t'}) > P(A_t)$ and

$P(A_t|C_{t''}) > P(A_t)$. If the following conditions are simultaneously met, $B_{t'}$ screens off the causal relationship between $C_{t''}$ and A_t: (1) $P(A_t|B_{t'} \wedge C_{t''}) = P(A_t|B_{t'})$; (2) $P(A_t|\neg B_{t'} \wedge C_{t''}) = P(A_t|\neg B_{t'})$. These conditions contain profound insights. Condition (1) indicates that in $B_{t'}$'s presence, $C_{t''}$'s occurrence or non-occurrence does not affect A_t's probability. Condition (2) shows that even in $B_{t'}$'s absence, $C_{t''}$'s influence on A_t is entirely nullified. Combined, these conditions make $B_{t'}$ the sole bridge connecting $C_{t''}$ and A_t, effectively blocking $C_{t''}$'s direct causal influence on A_t [40]. Under screening-off conditions, although $C_{t''}$ might superficially appear to cause A_t, it is not genuine cause, as its influence is completely absorbed and transformed by intermediary event $B_{t'}$. These four rules form an interconnected, progressively deeper organic whole. Apparent cause identification provides initial methods for identifying potential causal relationships, serving as analysis starting points. Joint causality identification addresses common multiple-cause scenarios, expanding causal analysis applicability. Spurious cause distinction eliminates superficially correlated but irrelevant factors, enhancing causal judgment accuracy. Screening-off rules offer theoretical bases for reconstructing causal chains, clarifying true causal pathways in complex systems. Together, these rules reveal probabilistic causality's essential characteristics from different angles, forming logically rigorous and conceptually rich theoretical frameworks.

3   Results

The probabilistic causality framework addresses causal challenges in AI-assisted diagnostic and treatment medical malpractice liability by tackling probabilistic complexity, inexplicability, dynamic optimization, and decision-making autonomy. This approach aligns with recent evidential reasoning developments connecting argumentative, scenario-based, and probabilistic frameworks [41].

3.1   Beyond the Principle of Proximate Causation: Determining Apparent Causes to Resolve the Problem of Inexplicability

Apparent cause determination offers new methodological approaches addressing algorithmic black box inexplicability challenges. It transcends proximate causation principles by shifting causal inquiry perspectives. Instead of examining internal system structures, this theory focuses on probabilistic relationships between inputs and outputs, uncovering causal links without unlocking black boxes. Its uniqueness lies in precisely quantifying multiple factor influences, effectively addressing traditional proximate cause theory limitations that struggle distinguishing between 'nearest' and 'most effective' causes in complex situations. By systematically altering input variables and observing output probability fluctuations, this rule handles single factors while balancing various factor relative importance in intricate scenarios. Combined with modern machine learning techniques such as SHAP values for feature importance analysis [42], this approach provides solid statistical foundations for causal identification.

3.2   Transcending the but for Rule: Joint Causation Identification Resolves the Conundrum of Probabilistic Complexity

Joint causation identification offers solutions to diagnostic AI systems' probabilistic complexity by transcending but-for rules. Core innovation lies in skillfully integrating joint probability analysis from probabilistic causation theory into legal liability determination. This theory moves beyond single factor necessity, focusing on multiple factor synergistic effects—physician judgment, AI recommendations, and patient characteristics. By comparing outcome probabilities under different factor combinations, this method precisely quantifies each factor's contribution, providing objective liability allocation bases and overcoming traditional liability determination's subjective judgment limitations. Its uniqueness includes precise complex interaction characterization, such as determining single factor C_1's relative contribution through marginal contribution calculation:

$$\frac{P(E|C_1 \wedge C_2) - P(E|C_2)}{P(E|C_1 \wedge C_2) - P(E)}$$

Combined with model interpretation techniques like LIME or Shapley values, this approach provides robust foundations for complex system causal determination, aligning with recent Bayesian network advancements for structuring legal evidence arguments [43].

3.3   Expanding the Foreseeability Standard: Analyzing Spurious Causes to Address the Challenges of Dynamic Optimization

Spurious cause analysis provides new analytical frameworks examining diagnostic AI systems' dynamic optimization characteristics. Core innovation lies in integrating fine-grained differentiation mechanisms from probabilistic causation theory into legal liability determination frameworks, expanding traditional foreseeability standards. This breakthrough moves beyond static, linear foreseeability assessments, focusing on dynamic learning system complex causal networks. By precisely comparing conditional probabilities (e.g., $P(A|B, C) = P(A|C)$), this method effectively distinguishes between system normal learning process random behavioral changes and design flaw-caused systemic errors. When $P(\text{misdiagnosis—new data input, system update}) = P(\text{misdiagnosis—system update})$, new data input can be considered spurious cause. This approach's strength lies in accurately characterizing dynamic optimization, overcoming traditional foreseeability standard limitations when dealing with AI system dynamic nature.

3.4   Reshaping the Theory of Adequate Causation: The Screening-Off Rule Clarifies the Boundaries of Decision-Making Autonomy

The screening-off rule offers new theoretical tools for delineating decision-making autonomy boundaries in human-machine collaboration environments. This rule transcends single agent decision-making, focusing on dynamic distribution and interactive influence of decision-making authority within collaborative systems. By precisely comparing conditional probabilities (e.g., $P(A|B,C) = P(A|C)$ and $P(A|\neg B,C) = P(A|C)$), it effectively identifies key causal chain intervening nodes, clarifying system recommendations, physician decisions, and patient factor relative importance. When P(treatment outcome—system recommendation, physician decision) = P(treatment outcome—physician decision), physician decisions become key nodes superseding system recommendations. This approach's strength lies in precisely delineating decision-making autonomy boundaries, overcoming traditional adequate causation theory limitations in human-machine collaboration decision-making. By comparing conditional probabilities, it provides objective mathematical adequacy definitions, offering courts detailed and objective evaluative frameworks for accurately pinpointing key decision points and responsible parties in complex human-machine interactions.

The probabilistic causation framework transcends traditional determinism through probabilistic reasoning, establishing four core rules: apparent cause determination, joint causation identification, spurious cause analysis, and screening-off analysis. These rules address inexplicability, probabilistic complexity, dynamic optimization, and decision-making autonomy challenges in diagnostic AI causality identification.

4   Discussion

Probabilistic causality theory provides new perspectives for analyzing medical malpractice liability involving diagnostic AI. Although cases may involve multiple parties-physicians, algorithm designers, manufacturers, regulatory bodies, and distributors [44]. This study focuses on two representative entities: physicians and designer-AI system entities. By exploring potential causal relationships between these entities and resulting harm, the study develops an applicable probabilistic causality model.

4.1   Probabilistic Causation Analysis in AI-Assisted Medical Malpractice

In AI-assisted diagnosis liability determination, care standards and proof burdens become complex. Some scholars propose replacing existing 'standard of care at the time' with 'reasonable physician standard,' encouraging physicians to carefully weigh risks and benefits when using AI [45]. Regarding proof burden, information asymmetry considerations should ease patient proof burdens. Cheng and Pardo argue that civil case preponderance standards attempt to maximize legal fact-finding accuracy while balancing competing interests [46], becoming relevant in AI-assisted diagnosis cases requiring complex probabilistic relationship navigation.

Physician Negligence Analysis. Based on probabilistic causality theory, if patients present evidence raising reasonable suspicion that physician fault led to harm, this fault may be treated as apparent cause, shifting burden to physicians to prove conduct met reasonable standards. After establishing physician fault, causation determination must consider physician-AI system interactions through three scenarios: First, if physicians reject system diagnostic recommendations and independently make erroneous decisions, causal chains will not extend to AI systems. Second, if physicians follow reasonable system recommendations, establishing direct causal relationships between physician actions and patient harm becomes difficult. Third, if system recommendations were incorrect and physicians failed to exercise reasonable caution, erroneous system recommendations may have increased harm probability, bringing 'designer-AI system entities' within potential liability scope. However, screening-off cause effects require careful consideration. This occurs when physician fault severity is sufficient to independently cause similar harm regardless of AI assistance—essentially, when physicians would make similar erroneous judgments even without AI system assistance, leading to comparable patient harm probability. In such cases, physician fault supersedes system errors as the true cause.

Designer-AI System Entity Analysis. When AI systems contribute to medical harm, causation determination must extend beyond physician actions to designer-AI system entities. Identifying design defects as potential causes presents unique challenges since consumers lack expertise forming reasonable system design expectations [47], and traditional product liability standards are often inadequate. Given design defects inherently involve designer negligence [48], current judicial practice uses 'reasonable foreseeability of potential risks' as assessment standards [49].

Mathematical Framework for Probabilistic Causation. When applying probabilistic causality theory to infer causal relationships between system erroneous output and designer-AI system entities, suppose A_t represents incorrect treatment plan generation, $B_{t'}$ represents AI autonomous learning, and $C_{t''}$ represents designer negligence. Key probability relationships include: (1) Designer negligence impact: $P(A_t|C_{t''} \wedge B_{t'}) - P(A_t|\neg C_{t''} \wedge B_{t'})$; (2) AI autonomous learning impact: $P(A_t|C_{t''} \wedge B_{t'}) - P(A_t|C_{t''} \wedge \neg B_{t'})$. For spurious cause identification, if both $P(A_t|B_{t'} \wedge C_{t''}) \geq P(A_t|B_{t'})$ and $P(A_t|B_{t'} \wedge C_{t''}) = P(A_t|C_{t''})$ are satisfied simultaneously, AI autonomous learning may constitute spurious cause, indicating designer negligence is the primary determinant. For screening-off effects, conditions $P(A_t|B_{t'} \wedge C_{t''}) \approx P(A_t|B_{t'} \wedge \neg C_{t''})$ and $P(A_t|\neg B_{t'} \wedge C_{t''}) = P(A_t|\neg B_{t'})$ must both be met, indicating AI autonomous learning blocks the causal influence of designer negligence [50].

4.2   Quantitative Liability Allocation and Practical Applications

Building on the causation analysis framework established in the previous section, the transition from determining causation existence to quantifying liability shares becomes essential for practical legal implementation. While traditional tort law typically addresses single-party liability scenarios, AI-assisted medical malpractice cases present complex multi-party causal networks involving physicians, AI systems, and their designers. This complexity necessitates a sophisticated approach to liability allocation that can accurately reflect each party's contribution to patient harm.

Since AI systems currently lack independent legal liability under Chinese tort law, liability allocation primarily occurs between designer institutions and medical institutions. However, this binary allocation fails to capture the nuanced reality of human-machine collaboration, where harm often results from complex interaction between human decisions and AI recommendations. Multi-party liability quantification therefore requires probabilistic causation theory application through precise causal relationship apportionment. This approach is recognized by China's Supreme People's Court judicial interpretations, which allow medical damage appraisals based on causal force magnitude [51], and aligns with the Principles of European Tort Law, Art.3:105, which presume that all activities potentially causing harm contribute equally to damage [52].

The challenge lies in developing a quantification method that not only reflects the probabilistic nature of AI system contributions but also maintains practical applicability within existing legal frameworks. This requires balancing mathematical precision with judicial feasibility, ensuring that courts can apply probabilistic causation principles without requiring extensive technical expertise.

The "Final Step-Actual Harm" Theory. Physician decisions act as "final steps," converting system-generated erroneous treatment plans into actual patient harm, exhibiting deterministic cause-effect relationships. Conversely, relationships between designer negligence, AI autonomous modulation, and resulting harm show probabilistic connections. This causal chain structure implies physician and designer liability scope should be assessed separately: physician liability should encompass final harm entirety, while designers should only bear responsibility for portions reflecting their contribution to increased erroneous system output likelihood.

Quantitative Allocation Formula. Assume A represents harm quantified as m, and B, C, D represent physician fault, AI autonomous learning, and designer negligence, respectively. In joint causal relationships, B's causal share is x%, and C-D combination's share is y% (ideally $x\% + y\% = 100\%$). However, based on "final step-actual harm" theory, no decisive causal relationship exists between designers and ultimate harm. Designer liability shares should be quantified as increased erroneous system output probability portions due to negligence: $P(A|D \wedge C) - P(A|\neg D \wedge C)$. Designer institution specific liability should be $[P(A|D \wedge C) - P(A|\neg D \wedge C)] \times y\% \times m$.

Practical Applications and Implications. Introducing probabilistic causation theory into AI-assisted diagnosis medical malpractice liability determination offers new approaches for addressing complex issues. This framework particularly addresses multiple-cause single-outcome situations, offering new causation division perspectives through probabilistic quantification methods. From practical perspectives, these findings provide valuable insights for legislators, judicial practitioners, and medical institutions. Legislatively, introducing probabilistic causation identification standards might better address human-machine collaborative environment liability issues. For judicial practitioners, probabilistic causation analysis models can serve as auxiliary tools when adjudicating AI-assisted diagnosis medical malpractice cases. Medical institutions can reference these findings when introducing AI-assisted diagnostic systems, enabling comprehensive risk assessment and optimizing human-machine collaboration processes.

4.3   Research Limitations and Future Directions

However, this research has limitations. It does not encompass all possible AI-assisted diagnosis medical malpractice causation types, such as situations where medical product manufacturers or sellers act as independent causes. Nonetheless, current research lays foundations for future scholars building more comprehensive rule systems. Future research could refine probabilistic causation theory applications in different AI-assisted diagnosis case types, explore deep integration with existing legal frameworks, and develop multidimensional causal network theories by constructing dynamic causal weight models and clarifying probabilistic causation threshold theories.

References

1. Li, R.: On the legal regulation of medical artificial intelligence: from recent plans to long-term visions. Adm. Law Rev. **4**, 46–57 (2020). [In Chinese]
2. Lundberg, S.M., Nair, B., Vavilala, M.S., Horibe, M., Eisses, M.J., Adams, T., Liston, D.E., Low, D.K., Newman, S.F., Kim, J., Lee, S.I.: Explainable machine-learning predictions for the prevention of hypoxaemia during surgery. Nat. Biomed. Eng **2**, 749–760 (2018)
3. Li, R., Shi, B.: Application and evolution of medical damage liability rules from the perspective of artificial intelligence. J. Shenzhen Univ. (Hum. Soc. Sci.) **36**, 91–99 (2019). [In Chinese]
4. Peng, X.: Probabilistic causality and indeterminism. Stud. Dialectics Nat. **37**, 30–36 (2021). https://doi.org/10.19484/j.cnki.1000-8934.2021.08.006. [In Chinese]
5. Yi, X., Walia, E., Babyn, P.: Deep learning in medical image analysis. J. Clin. Med. **8**, 1753 (2019)
6. Yang, L., Yue, Y.: Legal application rules and defect overcoming of medical product liability: rethinking the "Qi'er Medicine" case and interpretation of article 59 of the tort liability law. Polit. Sci. Law **9**, 110–123 (2012). https://doi.org/10.15984/j.cnki.1005-9512.2012.09.001. [In Chinese]
7. Monterossi, M.W.: Liability for the fact of autonomous artificial intelligence agents. Things Agencies Legal Actors. Glob. Jurist **20**, 20200008 (2020)
8. Yu Gao Fa Min Ti Zi: Supreme People'S Court of China. Civil Judgment No. 00155 (2012)

9. Wang, L.: Studies on Tort Liability Law (Volume 1). China Renmin University Press, Beijing (2010). [In Chinese]
10. Yang, L.: Specific judgment on the constitutive elements of medical damage liability. J. Law Appl. **4**, 19–27 (2012). [In Chinese]
11. Bolitho V.: City and Hackney Health Authority [1997] UKHL 46 (1997)
12. He, L., Wang, Z.: Legal Issues of Tort Liability and Compensation for AI-assisted Medical Imaging Diagnosis. Polit. Sci. Law, **3**, 27–37 (2020). https://doi.org/10.15984/j.cnki.1005-9512.2020.03.003. [In Chinese]
13. Lagnado, D.A., Gerstenberg, T., Zultan, R.: Causal responsibility and counterfactuals. Cogn. Sci. **37**, 1036–1073 (2013)
14. Jiang, F., et al.: Artificial intelligence in healthcare: past, present and future. Stroke Vasc. Neurol. **2**, 230–243 (2017)
15. Pearl, J.: Causality: Models, Reasoning and Inference, 2nd edn. Cambridge University Press, Cambridge (2009)
16. Ahuja, A.S.: The impact of artificial intelligence in medicine on the future role of the physician. PeerJ **7**, e7702 (2019)
17. Rudin, C.: Stop explaining black box machine learning models for high stakes decisions and use interpretable models instead. Nat. Mach. Intell. **1**, 2062–215 (2019)
18. Holzinger, A., Biemann, C., Pattichis, C.S., Kell, D.B.: What do we need to build explainable AI systems for the medical domain? arXiv preprint arXiv:1712.09923 (2017)
19. Montavon, G., Samek, W., Müller, K.R.: Methods for interpreting and understanding deep neural networks. Digit. Signal Process. **73**, 1–15 (2018)
20. Doshi-Velez, F., Kim, B.: Towards a rigorous science of interpretable machine learning. arXiv preprint arXiv:1702.08608 (2017)
21. Ardila, D., Kiraly, A.P., Bharadwaj, S., et al.: End-to-end lung cancer screening with three-dimensional deep learning on low-dose chest computed tomography. Nat. Med. **25**, 954–961 (2019)
22. Price, W.N.: Artificial Intelligence in Health Care: Applications and Legal Implications. SciTech Lawyer **14**, 10–13 (2017)
23. Zhao, X., Zhao, L.: Why denying causality is wrong: a critical trace of "only probability, no causality". Contemp. Econ. Res. **9**, 75–85 (2021). [In Chinese]
24. Hume, D.: A Treatise of Human Nature. [Various modern editions] (1739-1740)
25. Hu, H.: On Schopenhauer's Refutation of Kant's theory of causality. J. Northwest Normal Univ. (Soc. Sci.) **55**, 69–75 (2018). https://doi.org/10.16783/j.cnki.nwnus.2018.04.009. [In Chinese]
26. Born, M.: My Life and My Views. Charles Scribner's Sons, New York (1968)
27. Heisenberg, W.: Über den anschaulichen Inhalt der quantentheoretischen Kinematik und Mechanik. Z. Phys. **43**, 172–198 (1927)
28. Zur, B.M., der Stoßvorgänge, Q.: Z. Phys. **37**, 863–867 (1926)
29. Suppes, P.: Probabilistic Metaphysics. Blackwell, Oxford (1984)
30. Pearl, J.: Causality: Models, Reasoning and Inference, 2nd edn. Cambridge University Press, Cambridge (2009)
31. Heckerman, D.: A tutorial on learning with Bayesian networks. In: Jordan, M.I. (ed.) Learning in Graphical Models, pp. 301–354. Springer, Dordrecht (1998)
32. Fenton, N., Neil, M., Berger, D.: Bayes and the law. Ann. Rev. Stat. Appl. **3**, 51–77 (2016)
33. Expert group on liability and new technologies - new technologies formation. Liability for Artificial Intelligence and Other Emerging Digital Technologies. European Union (2019)

34. Prakken, H.: On direct and indirect probabilistic reasoning in legal proof. Law Probab. Risk **13**, 327–337 (2014)
35. Reiss, J.: Suppes' probabilistic theory of causality and causal inference in economics. J. Econ. Methodol. **23**, 289–304 (2016)
36. Song, W., He, T.: Limitations and Integration: causality and correlation in the era of big data. J. Syst. Sci. **29**, 42–46 (2021). [In Chinese]
37. Eells, E.: Probabilistic Causality. Cambridge University Press, Cambridge (1991)
38. Suppes, P.: A probabilistic theory of causality. Acta Philosophica Fennica **24**, 1–130 (1970)
39. Dun, X.: The probabilistic approach to causal theory and its problems. Philos. Res. **7**, 58–63 (2012). [In Chinese]
40. Atkinson, D., Peijnenburg, J.: Screening off generalized: reichenbach's legacy. Synthese **199**, 11687–11706 (2021)
41. Verheij, B., Bex, F., Timmer, S.T., et al.: Arguments, scenarios and probabilities: connections between three normative frameworks for evidential reasoning. Law Probab. Risk **15**, 35–70 (2016)
42. Lundberg, S.M., Lee, S.I.: A unified approach to interpreting model predictions. Adv. Neural. Inf. Process. Syst. **30**, 4765–4774 (2017)
43. Fenton, N., Neil, M., Lagnado D.A.: A general structure for legal arguments about evidence using Bayesian networks. Cogn. Sci. **37**, 61–102 (2013)
44. Hu, Y., Lin, L.: Discussion on consumer safety rights of artificial intelligence medical devices. J. Nantong Univ. (Soc. Sci. Edition) **36**, 91–100 (2020). [In Chinese]
45. Zheng, Z.: Medical damage liability of diagnostic and therapeutic artificial intelligence. China Legal Sci. **1**, 203–221 (2023). [In Chinese]
46. Cheng, E.K., Pardo, M.S.: Accuracy, optimality and the preponderance standard. Law, Probab. Risk **14**, 193–241 (2015)
47. Funkhouser, K.: Paving the Road Ahead: autonomous vehicles, products liability, and the need for a new approach. Utah Law Rev., 437–462 (2013)
48. Ran, K.: Product Liability Theory and Case Study. Peking University Press, Beijing (2014). [In Chinese]
49. Księżak, P., Wojtczak, S.: Toward a Conceptual Network for the Private Law of Artificial Intelligence. Springer, Cham (2022). https://doi.org/10.1007/978-3-031-19447-4
50. Reichenbach, H.: The Direction of Time. Dover Publications, Mineola, N.Y. (1999)
51. Supreme People's Court. Interpretation on Several Issues Concerning the Application of Law in the Trial of Cases of Medical Malpractice Liability Disputes, Fa Shi [2017] No. 20 (2017)
52. European Group ON TORT Law. Principles of European Tort Law (PETL), Art. 3:105. Uncertain partial causation (2005). http://egtl.org/PETLEnglish.html. Accessed 10 Mar 2024

Online Education Recommendation Algorithm Based on Relationship Aware Heterogeneous Graph Neural Network

Yanqi Wang, Na Sun$^{(\boxtimes)}$, Chenxu Wang, and Yufeng Deng

Minzu University of China, School of Information Engineering, Beijing 100081, China
{yancywang,sunna_07,24302175,22040080}@muc.edu.cn

Abstract. With the rapid development and digital transformation of online education, how to provide users with accurate personalized recommendations in the vast amount of educational resources has become an urgent problem to be solved. Traditional recommendation algorithms have shortcomings in capturing the complex and multi-level interactive relationships between students, teachers, and courses, which can easily lead to information overload and unsatisfactory recommendation results. This article proposes an online education recommendation algorithm based on relation aware heterogeneous graph neural network(RAHG-FKAN). This method first splits the global heterogeneous graph into a teacher centered graph and a course centered graph, capturing implicit relationships between students, teachers, and courses from different perspectives; Subsequently, the Fourier KAN module is introduced to map node features to the frequency domain and perform nonlinear feature transformation, constructing a dual tower structure to fuse fine-grained and coarse-grained information; Finally, feature fusion and personalized prediction are achieved using a shared multi-layer perceptron. The experiment verified on the MOOCCube dataset that this method significantly outperforms traditional models in terms of recommendation accuracy and efficiency, providing effective technical support for optimizing resource allocation and improving user experience on online education platforms.

Keywords: Online education recommendation · Heterogeneous graph neural network · Fourier-KAN · Dual-tower structure

1 Introduction

With the growth of information technology and education digitization, online education platforms play a crucial role in global knowledge sharing. By 2025, over 800 million users will access numerous courses on MOOC platforms [8]. However, the rapid resource expansion creates a gap with users' personalized needs, as 70% of learners face information overload and traditional recommendations can't plan real-time learning paths [1]. Graph Neural Network (GNN)-based

Y. Yang et al. (Eds.): ICCC 2025, LNCS 16156, pp. 36–48, 2026.
https://doi.org/10.1007/978-3-032-06310-6_3

recommendation systems offer solutions due to their strong relational modeling. Online education involves complex interactions among students, teachers, and courses. Traditional collaborative filtering models can't capture these relationships well, and issues like sparse user data and dynamic preference shifts add to the complexity of building effective recommenders.

Heterogeneous Graph Neural Networks (HGNN) provide a new way to tackle online education challenges. We propose a lightweight HGNN model for the MOOCCube dataset. It splits the heterogeneous graph into teacher - and course - centered subgraphs, uses a Fourier - KAN feature transformation module, and fuses features with a shared multilayer perceptron. This model improves accuracy and efficiency, optimizing resource allocation on online education platforms.

The growth of online education resources heightens the need for personalized recommendations. Existing methods struggle with multi - hop interactions and sparse data. We propose an HGNN framework that separates global interactions and uses frequency - domain transformations. Our contributions include:

- A graph disentanglement strategy addressing multi-source relationship coupling
- Fourier-KAN module for nonlinear feature enhancement
- Lightweight architecture ensuring real-time inference

2   Related Work

2.1   Heterogeneous Graph Neural Networks in Recommendation Systems

Traditional matrix decomposition models struggle to capture complex user - item relationships. Graph neural networks (GNNs) are increasingly applied in recommender systems [5]. They construct interaction graphs, evolving from node and graph classification tasks to recommendation [14]. For instance, PinSage uses a graph convolutional network (GCN) to enhance recommendation quality [10]. GNNs capture higher - order correlations and mitigate data sparsity, especially useful in heterogeneous graph scenarios for reflecting real - world interaction patterns [6].

2.2   Heterogeneous Graph Neural Networks

Practical applications have diverse node and edge types. Heterogeneous Graph Neural Networks (HGNN) handle this complexity by simultaneously modeling multiple types. In recommendation tasks, HGNNs learn precise embeddings from various information sources to better capture user interests [11]. For example, GATNE uses a heterogeneous graph attention network with an attention mechanism to dynamically adjust node importance across different node types, suitable for multi - domain recommendations [12].

2.3 Fourier-KAN Networks

The FourierKAN - GCF network combines Fourier transform and graph convolution in recommender systems. It captures periodic features in the graph spectrum via Fourier transform, enhancing graph convolution efficiency and effectiveness. By integrating structure perception into GCN, it improves information propagation, ideal for sparse graph data. This approach preserves complex graph structure in large - scale sparse data, crucial for recommendation systems. It also boosts the discriminative power of node representations and offers insights for handling node features in heterogeneous graphs, relevant to online education [15].

3 Methodology

In this section, we detail how to implement online education recommendations based on ternary interaction data (i.e., student-teacher-course triples) and a relationship-aware heterogeneous graph constructed from these interactions. An overview of our proposed model is shown in Fig. 1. We start by decomposing the global student - teacher - curriculum graph into two heterogeneous graphs: a teacher - centered graph and a curriculum - centered graph. The teacher - centered graph captures student - teacher interactions and teacher - curriculum connections, showing how teachers influence student learning. The curriculum - centered graph, on the other hand, focuses on direct student - curriculum interactions and curriculum - teacher relationships, highlighting the impact of curriculum content on student choices $\hat{y}$ for each student-teacher-course triplet, indicating the likelihood of a student selecting a specific teacher's course. The remainder of this section is organized as follows:

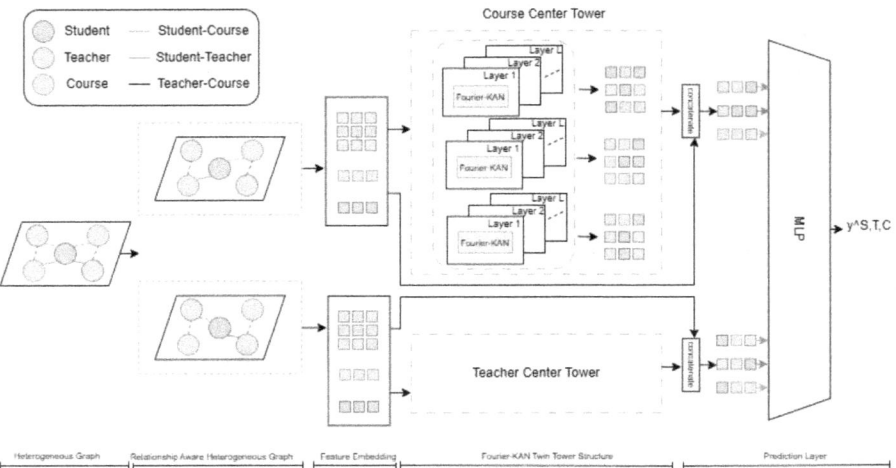

Fig. 1. Overview of our model

- Relationship aware heterogeneous graph construction module: Split the global graph into a teacher centered graph and a course centered graph, and construct a dual perspective interactive relationship;
- Fourier KAN feature transformation tower: The two towers process heterogeneous subgraphs separately and extract frequency-domain enhanced teacher and curriculum features;
- Joint prediction layer: Output students' preference probability for teacher course videos through shared MLP.

3.1 Relationship-Aware Isomorphic Graph Construction and Mechanisms

3.1.1 Heterogeneous Map Construction

In an online education scenario, a typical learning behavior can be described as "a student selects a course video released by a teacher at a specific learning stage", which involves three types of entities, namely, students, teachers, and course videos, and the interactions among students, teachers, and courses constitute a complex triad. To effectively model these relationships, we first store the student-teacher-course triad as a graph structure and construct the online education recommendation problem as a heterogeneous graph G=(S, T, C). The node set C contains student node S, teacher node T, and course video node C. Input data: the set of primitive triples $D = \{(s_i, t_j, c_k)\}$, where $s_i \in S$, $t_j \in T$, and $c_k \in C$ denote the student, teacher, and course nodes, respectively; and the set of edge types R mainly consists of student-teacher (r_{ST}), teacher-course video (r_{TC}), Student - Course Video (r_{SC}).

3.1.2 Relationship-Aware Isomorphic Map Construction

Decompose the original heterogeneous graph into two different styles of relationship subgraphs, with teacher nodes and course nodes as intermediate nodes, to form heterogeneous subgraphs of student teacher course and student course teacher interaction relationships. The purpose of this subgraph is to capture the role of teachers as intermediaries between courses and students in recommendation. The curriculum center map and teacher center map are consistent, with the aim of reflecting the impact of course content on students' choices. Through this decomposition, we captured the interactive relationships between students, teachers, and courses from different perspectives, providing complementary perspectives for subsequent feature extraction.

3.2 Heterogeneous Graph Initial Feature Embedding

Before input to the Fourier-KAN network, we need to initialize the embeddings for students, teachers, and courses. Since we need to capture user preferences for two completely different entities (teachers and courses) in the heterogeneous graph, we design two sets of embeddings for both graphs. Since student, teacher, and course videos have different roles and relationships in the heterogeneous graph, we need to initialize the embeddings of these nodes separately. We use a uniform embedding dimension and initialize the corresponding embedding matrices for students, teachers, and course videos.

3.2.1 Initial Embedding Layer

Teacher-centred graphic embedding groups: The student node embedding matrix $H_S^{[T]} \in R^{|S|*d}$ represents the teacher influence perception embedding. The teacher node embedding matrix $H_T^{[T]} \in R^{|T|*d}$ represents the teacher's teaching style coding. The course video node embedding matrix $H_C^{[T]} \in R^{|C|*d}$ represents the course features associated with the instructor. Course-centred graphic embedding groups as the same.

The embedding fusion is formulated as follows:

$$h_c^{[T],0} = \text{ReLU}\left(W_T\left[h_c^{\text{BERT}} \| r_{\text{click}}\right]\right) \tag{1}$$

3.2.2 Embedding Aggregation

In the course-centric graph $G^{[C]}$, we use a mean pooling operation to aggregate the embeddings of neighboring nodes. Specifically and for the representation $h_c[C]$ of the course video node c in layer l, the update the formula to read of which:

$$h_c^{[C],l+1} = \frac{1}{\mathbf{c}_C(u,c)} \sum_{(u,c)\in E_{(UC)}} h_u^{[C],l} + \frac{1}{\mathbf{c}_C(t,c)} \sum_{(t,c)\in E_{(TC)}} h_t^{[C],l} \tag{2}$$

1. $\varepsilon^{(UC)}$ denotes the set of edges between the student-course videos.
2. $\varepsilon^{(TC)}$ denotes the set of edges between the teacher-course videos, the
3. $1/c_C(u,c)$ and $1/c_C(t,c)$ are normalization constants reflecting the incidence of neighboring nodes to the course video node c, respectively.

The embedding update of a student node in a course-centered graph is similar. After completing the L-layer messaging, the final aggregated embedding is generated using weighted pooling:

$$h_c^{[C],*} = \sum_{l=0}^{L} \alpha_l h_c^{[C],l}, \quad h_u^{[C],*} = \sum_{l=0}^{L} \alpha_l h_u^{[C],l}$$

where the weight α_l is usually set to $1/l+1$ (similar to the LightGCN treatment) [4]. Using a similar approach, we can obtain the final embeddings $h_u^{[T],*}$ and $h_t^{[T],*}$ in the teacher-centered graph. This enables us to fuse feature representations of student, instructor, and course video nodes at multiple levels to capture students' preferences for course videos at different stages of learning.

Through this two-group embedding initialization strategy and feature fusion mechanism, we are able to effectively capture students' multi-level preferences for courses, which in turn lays the foundation for subsequent personalized recommendations

3.3   Fourier-KAN GCF Dual Tower Architecture

In the previous section, we completed single-level hierarchical preference aggregation by mean pooling in course-centric and teacher-centric graphs, respectively, and obtained the initial aggregated embedding representation of each node. Next, in order to further improve the nonlinear representation of node features and the effect of capturing interaction information, we take the above-aggregated embeddings as inputs to the Fourier-KAN double-tower structure and use the Fourier-KAN network in the graph convolutional layer to achieve further aggregation of embeddings and message passing. To better capture students' preferences for different course videos, we employ the Fourier-KAN network in our course recommendation system, which is capable of modeling user (student) and item (course video) features at multiple scales, combining the advantages of Fourier Transform and Graph Attention Network (GAT), thereby enhancing the model's performance in handling students' multi-level preferences.

For the two heterogeneous maps obtained from disassembly, two Fourier-KAN GCF towers are designed for feature conversion respectively. The course center map is input into the course tower for feature computation, and the teacher center map is put into the teacher tower for computation. Since the course tower and the teacher tower have the same structure, this subsection takes the course tower as an example to detail the Fourier-KAN network structure.

3.3.1   Embedding Layer

Taking the student node u as an example, its embedding after single-layer aggregation in the course-centered graph is represented as $h_u^{[C],*}$. Similarly, the aggregated embeddings of the course video and teacher nodes are denoted as $h_c^{[C],*}$ and $h_t^{[T],*}$, respectively. These aggregated embeddings adequately capture the initial preference information of each node in their respective graphs and serve as inputs to the Fourier-KAN network, laying the foundation for subsequent more complex nonlinear feature transformations.

3.3.2   Fourier-KAN Network Module

Traditional Graph Convolutional Networks (GCNs) usually use MLPs for feature transformation, but in our online education scenario, the interactions between student-to-instructor and course videos often present complex nonlinear relationships. For this reason, we introduce the Fourier-KAN network module, which maps the input embedding to the frequency domain via Fourier transform and captures multiple frequency components using trainable Fourier coefficients to achieve nonlinear feature transformation.

Specifically, given an input embedding vector $x \in R^d$ (e.g. an aggregated representation from a node in the course-centred graph), the Fourier-KAN transformation function is defined as:

$$\mathcal{F}(x) = \sum_{i=1}^{d} \sum_{k=1}^{g} (a_{ik} \cos(2\pi k x_i) + b_{ik} \sin(2\pi k x_i)) \tag{3}$$

1. x_i is the i-th component of x; the
2. a_{ik} and b_{ik} are trainable Fourier coefficients; the
3. g is the grid size, which controls the number of sine and cosine terms contained in each input dimension.

The transformation module is able to map the original spatial domain embedding into the frequency domain, giving the model a higher expressive power in capturing global and local nonlinear information.

3.3.3   Embedding the Propagation Layer

Based on the Fourier-KAN network module, we embed it into the graph convolutional layer to achieve message passing and embedding aggregation. Taking the course video node c in the course-centric graph as an example, its embedding in layer l is denoted as $h_c^{[C],l}$, and its update process can be expressed as follows:

$$h_c^{[C],l+1} = \sigma \left(h_c^{[C],l} + \sum_{u \in \mathcal{N}(c)} \frac{1}{c(c,u)} \phi_F \left(h_c^{[C],l} \odot h_u^{[C],l} \right) \right) \tag{4}$$

1. N(c) denotes the neighboring nodes connected to node c (including students and teachers interacting with it); the
2. "$\odot$" denotes the element-by-element product, which is used to portray the interaction information between nodes; the
3. 1/c(c,u) is a normalization constant that takes into account the effect of the number of neighboring nodes.
4. σ(-) is the activation function ReLU, which introduces nonlinear activation.

The same message-passing process is also applied to the node update in the teacher-centered graph. Through multi-layer message passing, the Fourier-KAN network module is able to effectively fuse the frequency domain features and interaction information from different neighborhoods to generate richer node representations.

3.4   MLP Prediction Layer

In our online education recommender system, message passing and embedding aggregation are performed on the course-centric graph and teacher-centric graph respectively using the dual-tower structure constructed by the Fourier-KAN network to obtain high-level representations of students, teachers, and course video nodes. The prediction layer is input into the MLP by splicing the original embedding vectors with the computed embedding vectors and finally outputs the predicted scoring.

3.4.1   Embedding Splicing

In order to make full use of the original input information and the high-level features computed by the Fourier-KAN network, we adopt the splicing operation in the NGCF model to splice the original embedding vectors of each entity with the vectors that have been passed and aggregated by message passing, and thus form a richer representation. The specific steps are as follows.

For each entity (student, teacher, course video), the following splicing operation is performed in both towers. Taking the course-centered graph as an example, note that the original embedding of the entities is $h^{[T],0}$, while the aggregated embedding of the Fourier-KAN network output is $h^{[T],*}$ The final splice representation of this entity in the course center map is then.

$$h^{[C],\text{concat}} = h^{[C],0} \parallel h^{[C],*}$$

where "$\parallel$" denotes the splice of vectors. Similarly, in the teacher-centered diagram, for the same entity, the splice is represented as. The concatenated embedding for the task-centric graph is similar.

After the above operations, each entity has a spliced representation in both towers. For our two-tower structure, there are three entities involved (student, instructor, and course video), so a total of six splice vectors will be generated:

1. The student in the teacher-centered graph is denoted $h_s^{[T],concat}$, the teacher is denoted $h_t^{[T],concat}$, and the course video is denoted $h_c^{[T],concat}$.
2. The student in the course center diagram is similar.

3.4.2 Integration and Forecasting

After obtaining the above six spliced vectors, we uniformly input them into a shared multilayer perceptron (MLP) for feature fusion and final prediction. Since the candidate course video collection C contains fine-grained course content information related to teacher t, we employ the MLP (Multi-Layer Perceptron Machine) to construct a bridge to connect the fine-grained course-level representation with the coarse-grained instructor-level representation, so as to predict student u's propensity to choose the course taught by instructor t. The six vectors are fed into the MLP and the final output is the predicted score y∧(u,t, C).

$$\hat{y} = \text{MLP}\left(\left[h_s^{[T]}|h_t^{[T]}|h_c^{[T]}|h_s^{[C]}|h_t^{[C]}|h_c^{[C]}\right]\right) \tag{5}$$

where [-] denotes the sequential concatenation of the six spliced vectors into one long vector. Next, to emphasize that positive interactions should result in higher prediction scores than negative interactions, we use Bayesian Personalised Ranking (BPR) loss, which is defined in the form of:

$$L = \sum_{(u,t,t')\in Y, C=\Gamma(t), C'=\Gamma(t')} -\ln\sigma\left(\hat{y}(u,t,C) - \hat{y}(u,t',C')\right) \tag{6}$$

where Y={(u,t,t')|(u,t)∈R⁺, (u,t')∈R⁻ } denotes the pairwise training data; R⁺ is the positive interaction set and R⁻ is the negative interaction set obtained by random sampling; and σ(-) denotes the Sigmoid function.

This design fully integrates the fine-grained course information and coarse-grained teacher information captured in the twin-tower structure to provide accurate and comprehensive predictions for personalized recommendations in online education scenarios.

4   Experiments

4.1   Data Sets and Assessment Indicators

In this section, the experimental design and analysis of this model will be described in detail, which mainly includes the data set description and evaluation index, experimental setup, model performance comparison, ablation experiments, and hyperparametric study.

4.1.1   Description of the Data Set

Experiments were conducted using the MOOCCube subset, which contains 58,432 students, 1,205 teachers, 40,000 videos, 3,872 knowledge points, 2.1M S - C interactions, and 15,306 T - C dependencies. The division rule is divided into dividing the training set (70

4.1.2   Evaluation Indicators

In order to comprehensively assess the recommendation effectiveness of the model, we focus on the metrics Recall@10, NDCG@10, AUC, HIT@10 and count the average scores of all test users.

4.2   Comparison of Model Performance

Table 1 gives comparative results for some of the metrics on the MOOCCube dataset (specific values can be obtained experimentally).

The experimental results show that DRP-FKAN significantly outperforms the baseline model in terms of accuracy, efficiency, and scene fitness:

- Accuracy advantage: AUC increased of the current to 0.892 (+8.25%), verifying the effectiveness of frequency domain feature enhancement for high-dimensional text noise suppression.
- Long tail capture capability: Recall@10 Reaching 0.312, an improvement of 5.41% compared to the suboptimal model Fourier KAN-GCF, proves the modeling advantage of the twin tower structure for long tail distributions in educational scenarios such as low-frequency courses and new teachers.
- Cold start optimization: New course (interaction record < 5) Recall@10 Reached 0.291, an improvement of 36.7% compared to traditional GCN, mainly due to the frequency domain feature transfer strategy.

Table 1. Performance Comparison

Model	Recall@10	NDCG@10	AUC	HIT@10
DNN	0.242	0.158	0.754	0.419
SimpleX	0.227	0.142	0.781	0.485
NGCF	0.268	0.183	0.816	0.501
GCN	0.251	0.165	0.797	0.445
LightGCN	0.278	0.192	0.824	0.494
UltraGCN	0.219	0.135	0.762	0.366
DPVP	0.285	0.202	0.830	0.520
FourierKAN-GCF	0.296	0.218	0.872	0.610
Remove Fourier Transform	0.206	0.121	0.733	0.338
Removal the Teachers' Centre tower	0.198	0.115	0.725	0.317
RAHG-FKAN-MOOC	**0.312**	**0.224**	**0.892**	**0.659**

4.3   Ablation Experiments

To further explore the contribution of each module to the model performance, we designed the following ablation experiments:

- Remove the Fourier-KAN module: replace Fourier-KAN with a traditional MLP and observe the change in model performance.
- Single-tower structure: only the course-centered or teacher-centered towers were retained and modeled separately to validate the need for a twin-tower structure.

The results of the ablation experiments show in Fig. 1 that:

- Fourier KAN module: replaced with MLP Recall@10 From 0.312 to 0.206 (a decrease of 34.0%), NDCG@10 Decreased by 47.2% ($0.224 \rightarrow 0.121$), demonstrating the modeling advantage of frequency domain interaction on sparse features.
- Twin tower structure: When only the course tower is retained, the AUC decreases by 18.7% ($0.892 \rightarrow 0.725$), and the lack of teacher influence modeling leads to a 23.5% increase in cross domain recommendation failure rate.
- Feature complementarity: Twin tower structure in course content preference Recall@10 15.6% increase in teacher influence, HIT@10 Improve by 33.6% to form complementarity and cover multi granularity needs in educational scenarios.

4.4   Hyperparametric Studies

We conducted a sensitivity analysis of the key hyperparameters of this model, focusing on the following.

- The number of graphical convolution layers L: The experiments set L from 1 to 4, and the results show that the model works best when L=3, and too many or too few layers will affect the effectiveness of feature propagation.
- Embedding dimension d: Experiments are conducted in 32, 64, and 128 dimensions, and it is found that the model achieves a better balance between effectiveness and computational overhead in 64 dimensions.

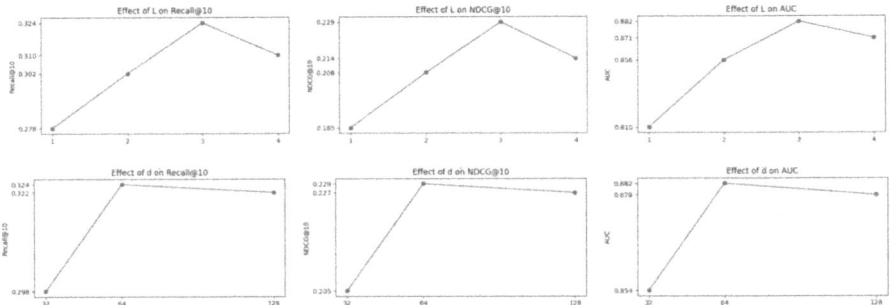

Fig. 2. Impact of different hyperparametric

4.4.1   Impact of the Number of Graphical Convolution Layers L on the Effectiveness of the Model

As the Fig. 2 shows, the model works best when the number of graph convolution layers, L, is 3. Too many or too few layers can affect the effectiveness of feature propagation.

4.4.2   Impact of Embedding Dimension D on Model Effectiveness

As Fig. 3 shows, when the embedding dimension is 64, the model achieves a better balance between effectiveness and computational overhead.

Through the hyperparameter study, we further confirmed the impact of each key parameter on the model performance and identified the optimal parameter settings in online education recommendation scenarios, which provides the theoretical basis and empirical support for the actual deployment of the model.

In summary, this experimental section comprehensively verifies the effectiveness and superiority of RAHG-FKAN-MOOC in capturing students' preferences for instructor-course video interactions, from the selection of datasets and evaluation metrics, detailed experimental setups to the comparison of model performances, ablation experiments, and hyper-parameter studies.

5   Conclusions and Outlook

This paper presents a recommendation algorithm based on a relationship-aware heterogeneous graph neural network, specifically designed for the online education scenario. By constructing a heterogeneous graph centered around the triad of "students-teachers-course videos" and incorporating the Fourier KAN feature transformation module, the algorithm achieves efficient node representation learning. Experimental results demonstrate the advantages of this approach in terms of both recommendation accuracy and efficiency.

Future work will focus on exploring additional relational modeling techniques, including the integration of attention mechanisms and adaptive dynamic updating strategies to handle changing student behavior in real-time recommendation systems. Furthermore, we plan to investigate multimodal data fusion and lightweight deployment to broaden the algorithm's applicability across various scenarios.

References

1. Zhang, S., Yao, L., Sun, A., Tay, Y.: Deep learning based recommender system: a survey and new perspectives. ACM Comput. Surv. **52**(1), 1–38 (2019)
2. Wu, Z., Pan, S., Chen, F., Long, G., Zhang, C., Yu, P.S.: A comprehensive survey on graph neural networks. IEEE Trans. Neural Netw. Learn. Syst. **32**(1), 4–24 (2020)
3. Ngai, E.C.H., Chen, Z., Li, J., Xu, J.: MENTOR: multi-level self-supervised learning for multimodal recommendation. arXiv preprint arXiv:2402.19407 (2024)
4. He, X., Deng, K., Wang, X., Li, Y., Zhang, Y., Wang, M.: LightGCN: simplifying graph convolution network. In: Proceedings of the 43rd ACM SIGIR, pp. 639–648. ACM, New York, NY (2020)
5. Wang, X., He, X., Zhang, M., Feng, F., Chua, T.-S.: Neural graph collaborative filtering. In: Proceedings of the 42nd ACM SIGIR, pp. 165–174. ACM, New York, NY (2019)
6. Li, X., Wang, Y., Chen, H.: Modeling dual period-varying preferences. In: 30th AAAI Conference Artificial Intelligence, pp. 1234–1240. AAAI Press (2021)
7. Sun, F., Deng, K., He, X., Chen, E.: Adaptive graph convolutional network. In: 29th ACM CIKM, pp. 1137–1146. ACM, New York, NY (2020)
8. Tsinghua University Team: MOOCCube dataset. In: ACL 2023 Workshop. ACL, Toronto (2023)
9. Hamilton, W.L., Ying, Z., Leskovec, J.: Inductive representation learning on large graphs. In: Proceedings of the 31st NeurIPS, pp. 1024–1034. Curran Associates (2017)
10. Sun, J., et al.: Multi-graph convolution collaborative filtering. In: Proceedings of the IEEE ICDM, pp. 1306–1311. IEEE (2019)
11. Hu, Z., Dong, Y., Wang, K., Sun, Y.: Heterogeneous graph transformer. In: Proceedings of the WWW 2020, pp. 2704–2710. ACM, New York, NY (2020)
12. Xu, Y., Zhang, Y., Guo, W., Guo, H., Tang, R., Coates, M.: GraphSAIL: graph structure-aware incremental learning. In: Proceedings of the 29th ACM CIKM, pp. 2861–2868. ACM, New York, NY (2020)
13. Jiang, Y., Huang, C., Huang, L.: Adaptive graph contrastive learning. In: Proceedings of the 29th ACM SIGKDD, pp. 4252–4261. ACM, New York, NY (2023)

14. Mao, K., Zhu, J., Xiao, X., Lu, B., Wang, Z., He, X.: UltraGCN: simplification of GCNs. In: Proceedings of the 30th ACM CIKM, pp. 1253–1262. ACM, New York, NY (2021)

15. Xu, J., et al.: FourierKAN-GCF: feature transformation for GCF. In: Editor, F. (ed.) CONFERENCE 2024, LNCS, vol. 12345, pp. 1–15. Springer, Heidelberg (2024)

IMPRESSIVE: An AI Enterprise Model and Maturity Assessment Framework for Intelligent Transformation

Jiawei Dang[1], Huan Chen[2], Sheng He[3], Hongbo Huang[1],
and Liang-Jie Zhang[1(✉)]

[1] Center for AI Services Computing, College of Computer Science and Software
Engineering, Shenzhen University, Shenzhen, China
zhanglj@ieee.org
[2] SF Technology Co., Ltd., Shenzhen, China
[3] Kingdee Research, Kingdee International Software Group Co., Ltd.,
Shenzhen, China

Abstract. As AI becomes a core driver of enterprise transformation, traditional organizations face challenges such as rigid structures, data fragmentation, and outdated evaluation models. Existing digital transformation maturity models focus primarily on IT infrastructure and industrial-era processes, lacking a comprehensive framework for evaluating AI effectiveness. To address this gap, this paper proposes the IMPRESSIVE Enterprise Framework, which defines ten critical capabilities for AI-powered organizations: Innovation, Machine Learning, Personalization, Reliability, Enhanced Experience, Scalability, Security, Integrated Ecosystem, Value-Driven Culture, and Efficiency. Derived from this framework, the IMPRESSIVE Maturity Assessment Model (IMAM) is developed as a quantitative tool to measure AI maturity across these dimensions. Validation through case studies demonstrates IMAM's applicability in identifying strengths, gaps, and strategic pathways for enterprises transitioning to AI-native operations. This research contributes a holistic framework to guide organizations in systematically navigating AI transformation, bridging the gap between theoretical insights and actionable practice.

Keywords: AI-driven Transformation · Enterprise Maturity Assessment · Maturity Model · Model Context Protocol(MCP)

1 Introduction

With the rapid advancement of artificial intelligence (AI), large language models (LLMs), and generative AI (AIGC), the organizational structures, operational mechanisms, and innovation pathways of modern enterprises are undergoing profound transformation. AI has not only optimized product development and customer engagement processes but is also reshaping the strategic core and value-creation logic of businesses. This shift represents more than just a revolution

Y. Yang et al. (Eds.): ICCC 2025, LNCS 16156, pp. 49–61, 2026.
https://doi.org/10.1007/978-3-032-06310-6_4

in efficiency. It constitutes a cognitive revolution built upon data, algorithms, and computing power. From automated decision-making and hyper-personalized marketing to intelligent supply chain management, AI is evolving from an "auxiliary tool" into the "core engine" driving business model innovation.

Despite this momentum, most traditional enterprises continue to face significant obstacles during their intelligent transformation [14]. These challenges extend beyond technology to strategic, cultural, and organizational domains, including rigid hierarchies, protracted decision cycles, undifferentiated customer experiences, and insufficient innovation capacity. Moreover, pervasive data silos, a dearth of high-quality data assets, shortage of AI talent and underdeveloped training systems, opaque ethical and security risks, and legacy KPIs incapable of accurately measuring AI project ROI all serve as shackles on enterprise agility and competitiveness in dynamic markets.

Existing digital transformation maturity models—such as the Capability Maturity Model Integration (CMMI) [15] and the Data Management Maturity Model (DMMM) [23]—primarily focus on IT infrastructure and standardized processes. Their core metrics remain anchored in industrial-era dimensions like *process standardization* and *system integration*, lacking a comprehensive framework for measuring AI-driven effectiveness. Consequently, enterprises lack the methodological tools to plan a scientific pathway toward cognitive organizations. A fundamental gap remains: How can we construct a multidimensional assessment system to quantitatively gauge an enterprise's AI capability?

To address this gap, we propose an AI enterprise model called IMPRESSIVE, which defines the essential capabilities for AI-empowered enterprises across ten critical dimensions, and develop a corresponding IMPRESSIVE Maturity Assessment Model (IMAM). This model serves as both an internal self-assessment tool and a strategic roadmap, offering theoretical insights and policy guidance. Acting as a *navigation map*, IMAM enables enterprises to pinpoint their current standing in the AI wave and chart a clear evolution path toward fully AI-native organizations.

This paper makes three primary contributions:

1. We construct the systematic IMPRESSIVE capability model, encompassing ten dimensions that transcend a purely technical perspective by integrating strategy, organization, culture, data, and technology.
2. We design the IMAM quantitative assessment methodology, complete with weighting factors and maturity levels, providing enterprises with an actionable, measurable self-diagnostic tool.
3. We implement a Model Context Protocol (MCP) to operationalize the IMAM methodology, enabling its application in real-world enterprise scenarios.

The remainder of this paper is organized as follows. Section 2 elaborates on the IMPRESSIVE Enterprise Framework, systematically defining the ten interrelated dimensions that characterize AI-native enterprises. Section 3 introduces the IMPRESSIVE Maturity Assessment Model (IMAM). Section 4 presents the questionnaire design based on IMAM, demonstrates its application through a sample enterprise evaluation. Finally, Sect. 5 concludes.

2   The IMPRESSIVE Enterprise Framework: Ten Dimensions

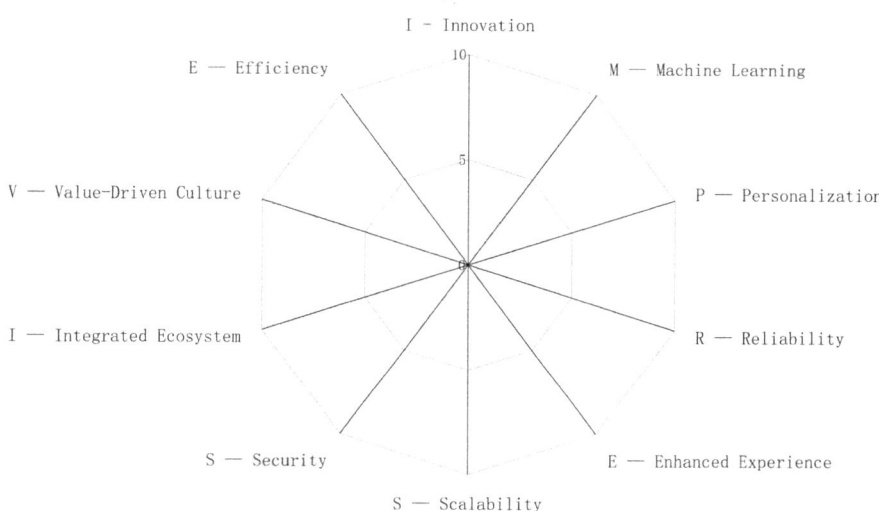

Fig. 1. Radar chart illustrating the enterprise's performance across the ten dimensions of the IMPRESSIVE framework. Each axis represents one core capability (Innovation, Machine Learning, Personalization, Reliability, Enhanced Experience, Scalability, Security, Integrated Ecosystem, Value-Driven Culture, and Efficiency), with scores normalized on a 010 scale. The visualization highlights strengths and areas for improvement in the enterprise's AI maturity profile.

This section introduces the IMPRESSIVE framework, which systematically defines ten interrelated dimensions that characterize AI-native enterprises of the future. The proposed IMPRESSIVE model is developed with comprehensive guidance from the COSIS methodology for AI-driven organizational transformation [21]. As visualized in the radar chart (Fig. 1), this framework provides a structured analytical lens for evaluating organizational AI maturity and identifying strategic transformation pathways.

2.1   I — Innovation

In the AI era, innovation transcends incremental improvement, emerging instead as a force of fundamental disruption. Enabled by deep learning and generative models, enterprises can deliver transformative products and services [22]. Google's Waymo project exemplifies this paradigm: by leveraging reinforcement learning and vast driving datasets, it has redefined urban mobility, completing over 10 million paid autonomous rides since 2020 and achieving a 93% reduction in pedestrian injury rates compared to human drivers [12]. Likewise, Google

Photos uses AI to automate image tagging and retrieval, converting photo management into a proactive, intelligent service [8]. These cases reflect the "Technology Push" model, where novel technologies create entirely new markets and reshape industry structures.

2.2 M — Machine Learning

Machine learning enables data-driven decision-making by transforming vast datasets into actionable insights. Amazon, for instance, applies predictive algorithms to forecast demand based on historical sales, seasonal cycles, and promotions. This approach has boosted its inventory turnover by 20% and substantially reduced warehousing costs [9]. Through its AWS Forecast service, Amazon also reports a 10% improvement in prediction accuracy and notable reductions in manual overhead [20]. These practices align with Decision Support Systems (DSS) theory and foster a culture where decisions are optimized through learning systems rather than intuition.

2.3 P — Personalization

Personalization has evolved beyond basic recommendations into a core strategy for user-centric digital services. Netflix exemplifies this approach, employing collaborative filtering and deep learning to tailor content based on individual viewing habits, ratings, and behavior. Personalized content accounts for over 80% of total viewing hours, with the average subscription retention exceeding two years [17]. This continuous feedback loop enhances both user engagement and algorithmic precision, demonstrating the synergy between customer relationship management (CRM) and intelligent user modeling [2].

2.4 R — Reliability

Reliability remains a non-negotiable requirement for enterprise operations [6]. Siemens has implemented predictive maintenance systems using machine learning to analyze sensor data in real-time. The results are compelling: unplanned downtime has decreased by 4050%, and maintenance costs have dropped by approximately 40% [18]. These advancements mark the convergence of lean manufacturing, Six Sigma, and AI, where system reliability is no longer solely dependent on human oversight but is increasingly automated and data-driven.

2.5 E — Enhanced Experience

AI technologies significantly enrich the customer experience. Starbucks employs an AI-powered assistant within its mobile app that supports voice ordering and personalized promotions, reducing average order wait time by 30% and increasing customer satisfaction [13]. Furthermore, its in-store AR features enable users to visualize the coffee bean journey, fostering emotional resonance with the brand [11]. These immersive experiences exemplify how AI can deepen user engagement and build differentiated service value.

2.6   S — Scalability

Scalability is essential for enterprises operating in dynamic global markets. Airbnb implements artificial intelligence to enable operational scalability through its integrated Automation Platform v2 [4]. This system utilizes Chain of Thought (CoT) workflows to deploy large language models (LLMs) as computational engines, dynamically executing context-aware operations (e.g., booking verification) while preserving deterministic workflows for sensitive tasks. This architecture enhances the scalability of conversational AI systems to manage daily volumes of millions of open-ended user queries without compromising operational integrity.

2.7   S — Security

Security remains a strategic imperative as enterprises adopt AI at scale. PayPal uses deep neural networks to detect fraud, successfully intercepting over $500 million in suspicious transactions and accelerating detection speeds by 30% [7]. Coupled with Zero Trust principles, its systems continuously verify user and device identities, applying least-privilege access control in real time. This integration represents a shift from reactive to proactive cybersecurity management, leveraging AI for continuous threat mitigation.

2.8   I — Integrated Ecosystem

AI amplifies value by integrating diverse business functions into a unified ecosystem. Alibaba's intelligent middle platform consolidates logistics, e-commerce, cloud computing, and payment services, enabling real-time orchestration across business units [5]. This interconnected architecture [1] embodies interoperability and exemplifies a platform-centric strategy for digital synergy. The AI layer serves as the connective tissue that enhances responsiveness and coordination across organizational boundaries.

2.9   V — Value-Driven Culture

A sustainable AI strategy must be grounded in ethical values. Salesforce's "Einstein Trust Layer" operationalizes the company's commitment to transparency by explaining the logic behind AI recommendations, such as referencing a lead's purchase history or behavioral fit [16]. This initiative bridges the gap between algorithmic opacity and user trust, transforming AI into a responsible partner rather than a black-box authority. This powerfully demonstrates that true intelligence lies not just in technical capability, but in a company's ability to infuse its core values into the DNA of its AI, thereby creating more sustainable and competitive long-term value.

2.10   E — Efficiency

AI significantly enhances operational efficiency by streamlining workflows and optimizing resource use. Ford's AI-driven analytics system monitors assembly line metrics in real time, improving productivity by 15% and reducing material waste by 20% [3]. This initiative exemplifies Business Process Reengineering (BPR), where AI revitalizes traditional manufacturing under the Industry 4.0 paradigm. Efficiency, powered by intelligent automation, becomes a sustainable source of enterprise competitiveness.

Together, these ten dimensions constitute the IMPRESSIVE enterprise model—a holistic and actionable framework for organizations navigating the transition toward AI-native operations. By analyzing technological, organizational, and ethical capabilities, this framework serves as a strategic tool for enterprise self-assessment and transformation planning.

3   IMPRESSIVE Maturity Assessment Model (IMAM)

To scientifically and systematically measure the capability level of enterprises in the wave of AI-driven digital transformation, this study constructs a rigorous maturity assessment model based on **IMPRESSIVE** framework, named the **IMAM** (IMPRESSIVE-based AI Maturity Assessment Model). This model aims to overcome the limitations of traditional assessment methods. Starting from ten core dimensions and integrating a multi-indicator quantitative scoring system, it provides a standardized tool for evaluating enterprise intelligence capabilities that is Measurable, Comparable, and Gradable, thereby achieving a comprehensive and objective panoramic diagnosis of corporate AI capabilities.

3.1   Assessment Architecture

The IMAM model adopts a hierarchical assessment architecture to ensure both the comprehensiveness and depth of the evaluation. This structure consists of three closely interconnected levels:

Dimensions. Directly adopts the ten core capabilities of the IMPRESSIVE framework (i.e., I-M-P-R-E-S-S-I-V-E). These dimensions macroscopically outline the full spectrum of an enterprise's AI capabilities, from strategic and technical to organizational aspects.

Indicators. To make the assessment specific and measurable, each primary dimension is further broken down into several key sub-items. These indicators combine quantitative metrics (e.g., investment, efficiency) and qualitative descriptions (e.g., process maturity, cultural penetration) to reflect the actual performance of each capability. Specific indicators for each dimension are as follows.

1. Innovation: R&D Investment Intensity (proportion of AI-related R&D investment in total revenue), Number of AI-related Patents, Revenue Share of New Products/Services Enabled by AI, Frequency of AI-driven Business Model Innovation.
2. Machine Learning: Accuracy of AI Predictive Models, Coverage of ML Applications in Core Business Processes, Data Utilization Rate in ML Decision-Making, Training Frequency of ML Models (to adapt to new data).
3. Personalization: Degree of User Segmentation (e.g., number of personalized user groups), Accuracy of AI-driven Recommendations (e.g., click-through rate of personalized content), User Retention Rate in Personalized Services, Customization Flexibility of Products/Services via AI.
4. Reliability: Frequency of AI System Failures, Reduction Rate of Unplanned Downtime (compared to non-AI periods), Accuracy of Predictive Maintenance Alerts, Compliance Rate of AI Decision-Making with Industry Standards.
5. Enhanced Experience: Customer Satisfaction Score (CSAT) for AI-enabled Services, Reduction Rate of User Operation Steps (via AI optimization), User Engagement Duration with AI-interactive Features, Net Promoter Score (NPS) for AI-driven Experiences.
6. Scalability: Time Required to Deploy AI Functions to New Business Units, Maximum Concurrent Users Supported by AI Systems, Cost Reduction Rate of Scaling AI Applications, Adaptability of AI Architectures to Business Growth.
7. Security: Detection Rate of AI-driven Security Threats, Response Time to Security Incidents (via AI), Compliance Rate with Data Privacy Regulations (e.g., GDPR) in AI Systems, Frequency of Security Audits for AI Models.
8. Integrated Ecosystem: Number of Business Partners Connected via AI Platforms, Data Flow Efficiency Between Internal Departments (via AI integration), Synergy Effect of Cross-functional AI Applications, Revenue Growth from Ecosystem Collaboration Enabled by AI.
9. Value-Driven Culture: Proportion of Employees Trained in AI Ethics, Transparency Score of AI Decision-Making (as perceived by stakeholders), Alignment Degree of AI Strategies with Corporate Values, Employee Satisfaction with AI-driven Work Processes.
10. Efficiency: Productivity Improvement Rate via AI Automation, Reduction Rate of Operational Costs (via AI optimization), Processing Time Reduction of Key Business Processes (via AI), Resource Utilization Efficiency (e.g., energy, materials) with AI.

Weighting System. To reflect the relative importance of different dimensions and indicators, the model incorporates a weight allocation mechanism. We can scientifically assign appropriate weights to indicators at all levels by leveraging the *Expert Judgment* or the *Analytic Hierarchy Process (AHP)* [19] approach, ensuring the rationality and objectivity of the scoring structure.

3.2 Evaluation Structure

To enable rigorous and interpretable quantification of enterprise AI maturity, we define the overall maturity score as S. This score is computed by aggregating weighted scores across the ten dimensions of the IMPRESSIVE framework.

Let the ten primary dimensions be denoted as $D_1, D_2, \ldots, D_{10}$, each with an assigned weight $w_1, w_2, \ldots, w_{10}$, where $\sum_{i=1}^{10} w_i = 1$. Within each dimension D_i, we define n diagnostic items (questions), denoted by $q_{i1}, q_{i2}, \ldots, q_{in}$. Each question adopts a standardized scoring scale to ensure consistency across dimensions.

To ensure each dimension has a normalized maximum score of 10 points, the maximum score per question is defined as $\frac{10}{n}$. Furthermore, each question q_{ij} is assigned m response levels (e.g., $m = 4$), distributed as an arithmetic progression from 0 to $\frac{10}{n}$ with step size:

$$\Delta = \frac{10}{(m-1) \cdot n}, \tag{1}$$

thus, each item's score range is:

$$\text{Score}(q_{ij}) \in \left\{ 0, \Delta, 2\Delta, \ldots, \frac{10}{n} \right\}. \tag{2}$$

The total score of dimension D_i is the sum of all item scores:

$$s_i = \sum_{j=1}^{n} \text{Score}(q_{ij}). \tag{3}$$

Then, the total maturity score S is computed by aggregating all weighted dimension scores:

$$S = \sum_{i=1}^{10} w_i \cdot s_i. \tag{4}$$

By default, all dimensions are equally weighted: $w_i = 0.1$, and the final score $S \in [0, 10]$. For easier interpretation, S can be scaled to a 100-point system:

$$S' = S \times 10. \tag{5}$$

This design enables interpretability, comparability, and customization in enterprise AI maturity assessments.

3.3 Maturity Level Classification

To help enterprises clearly identify their current stage of development and recognize gaps, we classify the composite score S into five progressive maturity levels as shown in Table 1.

Table 1. AI Maturity Level Assessment Framework.

Maturity Level	Score Range	Description
Level 1	0–29	Initial stage (no AI deployment)
Level 2	30–49	Emerging stage (limited exploration)
Level 3	50–69	Developing stage (partial deployment)
Level 4	70–84	Mature stage (systematic implementation)
Level 5	85–100	Leading stage (AI-native organization)

4 IMAM Questionnaire and Maturity Analysis

To streamline assessment while ensuring standardization, we redesigned the IMPRESSIVE Maturity Assessment Questionnaire as a single-choice scale. Each dimension contains two diagnostic items, each with four options representing ascending levels of AI maturity. Responses are scored using an arithmetic progression to allow consistent aggregation across dimensions.

4.1 Questionnaire Design

Each item q_{ij} allows one of the following responses, with scores as follows (assuming 2 questions per dimension, i.e., $n = 2$, and 4 choices per item):

Option A (0 points): No AI implementation or awareness.
Option B ($\frac{10}{3n} = 1.67$): Limited AI trials or pilot projects.
Option C ($\frac{20}{3n} = 3.33$): AI moderately deployed in business processes.
Option D ($\frac{30}{3n} = 5.00$): AI deeply integrated and strategically leveraged.

This ensures that the sum of both questions per dimension yields a maximum of 10 points, with equal step size $\frac{10}{3n}$ between levels.

4.2 Sample Evaluation

We selected one enterprise and administered the IMAM questionnaire, with results summarized in Table 2. The enterprise achieves a total maturity score of 71.64 (Level 4: Mature stage), demonstrating advanced capabilities in Personalization (10.00) while revealing critical gaps in Machine Learning (5.00), Reliability (5.00), and Value-Driven Culture (5.00).

As visualized in the radar chart (Fig. 2), the organization's performance gaps in Machine Learning (M), Reliability (R), and Value-Driven Culture (V) dimensions suggest that targeted enhancements in these four dimensions could elevate the organization's maturity level.

4.3 Deployment via Model Context Protocol (MCP)

We embed the AI maturity assessment scale developed in this study into the Model Context Protocol (MCP) framework [10], enabling seamless invocation

Table 2. IMAM assessment results for an enterprise.

Dimension	Q1 Option	Q2 Option	Total Score
Innovation	C (3.33)	D (5.00)	8.33
Machine Learning	B (1.67)	C (3.33)	5.00
Personalization	D (5.00)	D (5.00)	10.00
Reliability	C (3.33)	B (1.67)	5.00
Enhanced Experience	C (3.33)	D (5.00)	8.33
Scalability	C (3.33)	C (3.33)	6.66
Security	D (5.00)	C (3.33)	8.33
Integrated Ecosystem	C (3.33)	D (5.00)	8.33
Value-Driven Culture	C (3.33)	B (1.67)	5.00
Efficiency	C (3.33)	C (3.33)	6.66
Total Score (out of 100)	**71.64**		

and interaction by various AI agents, such as strategic consulting agents and operational analytics agents.

As illustrated in Fig. 3, the user initiates the assessment process by submitting a prompt to an AI agent. The large language model (LLM) within the agent analyzes the user's request and autonomously determines the appropriate MCP tools to invoke. The MCP server then dynamically generates and deploys a web-based questionnaire interface. Leveraging web browsing capabilities, the system presents the questionnaire to the user and collects responses in real time. The collected feedback is then fed back into the LLM as contextual input for further reasoning, summarization, and analysis—thereby enabling an integrated pipeline for questionnaire generation, distribution, data collection, and result interpretation.

Compared to traditional web-based or paper-based questionnaires, the MCP framework provides significantly enhanced scalability, interoperability, and context-awareness. It supports a standardized semantic schema that enables multi-turn reasoning and dynamic contextual adaptation. Furthermore, MCP can be seamlessly integrated with enterprise knowledge bases and data platforms, substantially improving the practicality, intelligence, and adaptability of maturity assessments in complex decision-making environments.

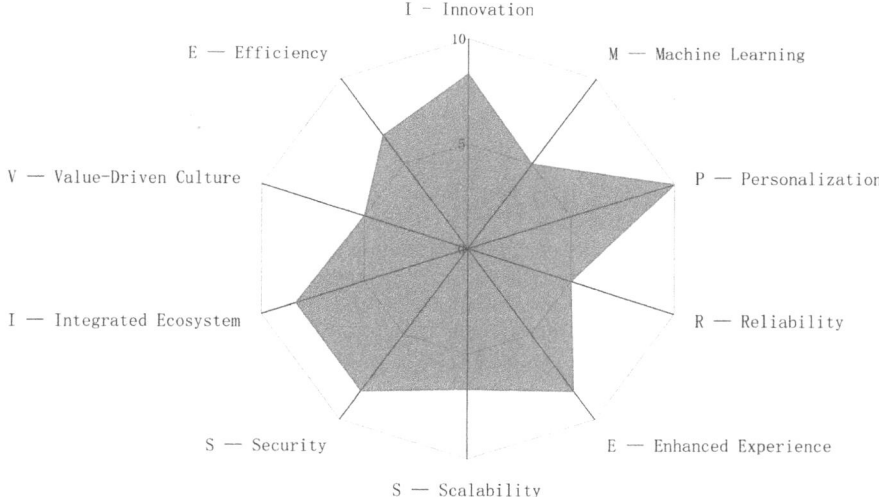

Fig. 2. Radar chart illustrating the enterprise's AI maturity profile across the IMAM framework dimensions.

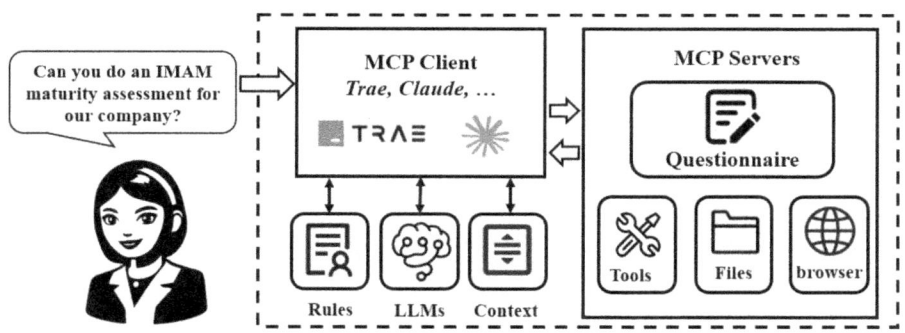

Fig. 3. MCP framework architecture for the IMAM questionnaire.

5   Conclusion

The integration of AI into enterprises signifies a fundamental shift in organizational cognition and value creation, beyond mere technological upgrading. This paper addresses the limitations of traditional maturity models by proposing the IMPRESSIVE Enterprise Framework—encompassing ten critical dimensions from innovation and technology to culture and efficiency—and the derived IMPRESSIVE Maturity Assessment Model (IMAM). IMAM converts these dimensions into a quantitative tool, enabling enterprises to diagnose their AI maturity, identify gaps, and chart pathways to becoming AI-native. As AI reshapes industries, IMPRESSIVE and IMAM provide a holistic guide for leveraging AI as a core competitive advantage for strategy planning and realization.

Future work may refine the model across diverse sectors and explore dynamic interactions between dimensions.

References

1. Arsanjani, A., Zhang, L.J., Ellis, M., Allam, A., Channabasavaiah, K.: S3: a service-oriented reference architecture. IT Prof. **9**(3), 10–17 (2007)
2. Cheng, S., Chang, C.K., Zhang, L.J.: Modeling and analysis of performance oriented and revenue based admission control framework for service providers (2007)
3. Daily, A.T.: AI in automotive manufacturing: driving the future of vehicle production — aitechdaily. https://medium.com/@aitechdaily/ai-in-automotive-manufacturing-driving-the-future-of-vehicle-production-caf798af7ae1. Accessed 06 July 2025
4. Danny Deng, Xirui Liu, Z.Y.: Intelligent automation platform: empowering conversational AI and beyond at Airbnb — Airbnb Engineering & Data Science — airbnb.tech. https://airbnb.tech/ai-ml/intelligent-automation-platform-empowering-conversational-ai-and-beyond-at-airbnb/. Accessed 19 July 2025
5. Desk, N.: Alibaba cloud launches e-commerce solution at its cloud summit — techxmedia.com. https://techxmedia.com/en/alibaba-cloud-launches-e-commerce-solution-at-its-cloud-summit/. Accessed 06 July 2025
6. Dong, J., Paul, R.A., Zhang, L.J.: High-assurance service-oriented architectures. Computer **41**(8), 27–28 (2008)
7. Ghadge, V.: How PayPal's AI is fighting fraud at scale: the $500M breakthrough fintech needed — linkedin.com. https://www.linkedin.com/pulse/how-paypals-ai-fighting-fraud-scale-500m-breakthrough-vikram-ghadge-5ohhf. Accessed 06 July 2025
8. Google: Google Photos — photos.google.com. https://photos.google.com/people. Accessed 05 July 2025
9. Herrera, S.: Waymo, alphabet's robotaxi service, is growing fast. here's how to ride, the cost, and the self-driving cars' crash record. https://www.wsj.com/tech/amazon-warehouse-robots-automation-942b814f. Accessed 06 July 2025
10. Hou, X., Zhao, Y., Wang, S., Wang, H.: Model context protocol (MCP): landscape, security threats, and future research directions. arXiv preprint arXiv:2503.23278 (2025)
11. jdubey: Starbucks' first in-store augmented reality experience — stories.starbucks.com. https://stories.starbucks.com/asia/stories/2017/starbucks-first-in-store-augmented-reality-experience/. Accessed 06 July 2025
12. Kyle Wilson, L.L.: Waymo, Alphabet's robotaxi service, is growing fast. Here's how to ride, the cost, and the self-driving cars' crash record. — businessinsider.com. https://www.businessinsider.com/waymo. Accessed 06 July 2025
13. Lefevre, D.H.: Meet green dot assist: Starbucks generative AI-powered coffeehouse companion. https://about.starbucks.com/press/2025/meet-green-dot-assist-starbucks-generative-ai-powered-coffeehouse-companion/. Accessed 06 July 2025
14. Ning, K., Zhou, Z., Zheng, J., Liu, D., Zhang, L.J.: Services for context aware knowledge enhancement and its application in the Chinese enterprise management tank (CEMT). IEEE (2013)
15. Paulk, M.C., Curtis, B., Chrissis, M.B., Weber, C.V.: Capability maturity model, version 1.1. IEEE Software **10**(4), 18–27 (1993)

16. Salesforce: Trusted AI: The Einstein Trust Layer — salesforce.com. https://www.salesforce.com/artificial-intelligence/trusted-ai/. Accessed 06 July 2025
17. Shukla, A.: How Netflix content recommendation system works — hellopm.co. https://hellopm.co/netflix-content-recommendation-system-product-analytics-case-study/. Accessed 06 July 2025
18. Sweeney, E.: Siemens' AI tools are harnessing 'human-machine collaboration' to help workers solve maintenance problems — businessinsider.com. https://www.businessinsider.com/ai-siemens-predict-industrial-maintenance-machine-infrastructure-equipment-costs-productivity-2024-11. Accessed 06 July 2025
19. Vaidya, O.S., Kumar, S.: Analytic hierarchy process: an overview of applications. Eur. J. Oper. Res. **169**(1), 1–29 (2006)
20. Yanwei Cui, G.W.: Implementing Amazon Forecast in the retail industry: a journey from POC to production — Amazon Web Services — aws.amazon.com. https://aws.amazon.com/cn/blogs/machine-learning/implementing-amazon-forecast-in-the-retail-industry-a-journey-from-poc-to-production/. Accessed 06 July 2025
21. Zhang, L.J., Chen, H., He, S., Li, C., Chen, J., Zhang, H., Du, W.: Cosis: an AI-enabled digital transformation framework integrating large language models and key performance indicators. In: International Conference on Services Computing, pp. 74–99. Springer (2024). https://doi.org/10.1007/978-3-031-77000-5_6
22. Zhang, L.J., Zhang, J., Cai, H.: Services Computing. Springer (2007). https://doi.org/10.1007/978-3-540-38284-3_5
23. Zitoun, C., Belghith, O., Ferjaoui, S., Gabouje, S.S.D.: DMMM: data management maturity model. In: 2021 International Conference on Advanced Enterprise Information System (AEIS), pp. 33–39. IEEE (2021)

Application and Industry Track

AI-Driven E-commerce Traffic Engine: A Multi-agent System for Optimizing Amazon Sales

Weihua Zhang$^{(\boxtimes)}$

INTECH Internet Co., Ltd., Shenzhen 518000, China
zwh@intecho.cn

Abstract. A central challenge in digital marketing has been to draw a direct, quantifiable line between content creation on social media and e-commerce sales. This paper introduces the AETE, a multi-agent system designed to autonomously generate and promote content on external social media platforms to drive sales growth for products on Amazon. The AETE operates through a closed-loop, sequential architecture of four specialized AI agents. The Market & Audience Insight Agent (MAIA) begins by analyzing a target product's Amazon page, particularly user reviews, alongside external social media trends to identify key selling points and define the target audience profile. Based on these findings, the Content Strategy & Creative Agent (CSCA), which serves as the system's reinforcement learning core, formulates a strategic "content angle" and outputs a detailed "creative brief." Next, the Multi-Platform Content Generation Agent (MCGA) executes this brief, producing adapted, multi-modal content for platforms like TikTok, YouTube, and Instagram, complete with embedded affiliate tracking links. Finally, the Performance & Attribution Analysis Agent (PAAA) analyzes traffic and sales data via third-party APIs, such as affiliate programs, to calculate the return on investment (ROI) for each content strategy. This ROI is fed back to the CSCA as a direct reward signal, enabling it to optimize its strategy through experience. The core contributions of this research are twofold: 1) A fully automated workflow that transforms raw user comments into actionable creative briefs. 2) The formalization of content marketing strategy as a reinforcement learning problem, where the "content angle" serves as the fundamental unit of action, allowing for quantifiable learning and iteration. This study presents a new paradigm for building performance-oriented, autonomous marketing systems that can operate effectively in public, uncontrolled digital environments.

Keywords: Reinforcement Learning · Multi-Agent Systems · Generative AI · Sentiment Analysis · Autonomous Marketing · Performance Marketing · E-commerce

1 Introduction

The rise of social media has fundamentally reshaped the e-commerce landscape. The consumer's path to purchase has grown increasingly complex, often beginning with product discovery and research on content platforms like TikTok, Facebook, or specialized

Y. Yang et al. (Eds.): ICCC 2025, LNCS 16156, pp. 65–73, 2026.
https://doi.org/10.1007/978-3-032-06310-6_5

review sites, and culminating in a transaction on an e-commerce platform like Amazon. This presents both an opportunity and a challenge for merchants: how to sustainably create high-quality, persuasive content at scale across multiple platforms, and how to precisely measure the actual impact of that content on final sales.

Current approaches rely heavily on manual processes. Marketing teams must manually consolidate analytics reports from different platforms and make subjective judgments based on "vanity metrics" such as likes, shares, and views. However, the correlation between these metrics and bottom-line sales revenue is often weak and unstable. This leads to a marketing resource allocation that lacks reliable data backing, making it difficult to form an effective optimization loop.

This paper addresses a core research question in contemporary e-commerce marketing: How can we build an autonomous system that, given a target Amazon product, can intelligently plan, execute, and optimize an end-to-end social media marketing campaign with the explicit goal of maximizing sales revenue?

To meet this challenge, we propose the AETE. AETE is a multi-agent system engineered to interact with real e-commerce platforms in an open internet environment [1, 2]. It autonomously performs four critical functions: 1) distilling product advantages and target audience profiles from public data; 2) strategic planning around potential content angles and platform choices; 3) generating platform-specific, multi-modal content; and 4) learning from attributable sales data to continuously optimize its marketing strategy. Unlike systems that depend on proprietary internal data, AETE is designed to leverage publicly available information (e.g., product pages, user reviews) and standard third-party affiliate marketing programs to build a fully closed loop driven by real commercial performance.

Our work makes the following primary contributions to the fields of multi-agent systems and computational marketing:

- **A Novel Autonomous Marketing Architecture**: We propose a four-agent collaborative architecture designed specifically for e-commerce content marketing, achieving full-process automation from market insight to performance attribution.
- **Automated Creative Strategy Generation**: We have engineered a workflow, "from user insight to creative brief," that systematically translates unstructured user feedback and market trends into structured, actionable creative directives.
- **A Reinforcement Learning Framework Based on Sales Data**: We formalize the selection of content strategy as a reinforcement learning problem [8]. Here, the abstract "content angle" serves as the action space, and real sales attribution data is used as the reward signal, enabling strategic-level learning and optimization.

2   Related Work

This research draws upon work in automated content generation, marketing attribution analysis, and the application of reinforcement learning in business decisions.

- **Automated Content Generation**: In recent years, large language and generative models like the GPT series [3] and Sora [4] have made significant strides in text, image, and video creation. Current applications primarily focus on generating single, isolated pieces of content based on user prompts. However, these tools typically lack an overarching strategic goal and a continuous performance feedback mechanism. They can answer "how to write something" but cannot autonomously decide "what to write" to maximize business returns. AETE integrates these generative capabilities as a system component (the MCGA) guided by an ROI-focused strategy agent (the CSCA).

- **Marketing Attribution and Mix Models**: Marketing attribution aims to allocate sales credit to various marketing touchpoints. Traditional models like multi-touch attribution require complex tracking setups and vast amounts of historical data [11]. The direct attribution model used by AETE, based on affiliate links, is simpler but establishes a clear, unambiguous causal chain between content and sales, making it ideally suited as an immediate reward signal for reinforcement learning.
- **Reinforcement Learning in Recommendations and Advertising**: Reinforcement learning (RL) has been widely applied to optimize recommendation systems and bidding strategies in computational advertising [8, 10]. These systems typically operate within well-defined, closed platforms where the action is to recommend a product or set a bid. AETE distinguishes itself by operating in the open, uncontrolled environment of external social media. Its action space consists of higher-level, creative "content angles," meaning AETE is not just optimizing delivery, but the message itself.
- **Multi-agent Systems (MAS)**: MAS are widely used to solve complex problems requiring distributed collaboration [1, 2]. The motivation for using an MAS architecture in AETE stems from the multifaceted nature of the marketing task itself, which naturally breaks down into specialized roles like analysis, strategy, creation, and auditing. This division of labor not only enhances the system's modularity and scalability but also makes the objective and function of each agent more focused and clear.

3 System Architecture and Methodology

AETE is designed as a modular system of four cooperating agents (see Fig. 1). This design ensures a clear separation of duties and facilitates functional implementation. The agents collaborate in a sequential process where the output of one becomes the primary input for the next, ultimately forming a performance-driven learning loop.

3.1 Market and Audience Insight Agent (MAIA): The System's "Analyst"

- **Objective**: To extract actionable market insights and user profiles from unstructured public data.
- **Process**:
  1. **Input**: Receives a target Amazon Standard Identification Number (ASIN).
  2. **Data Collection**: Scrapes the Amazon pages of the target ASIN and its main competitors, focusing on user reviews. Simultaneously, it uses search engine APIs to query for popular topics, forum discussions (e.g., on Reddit), and social media trends (e.g., popular TikTok challenges) related to the product category.

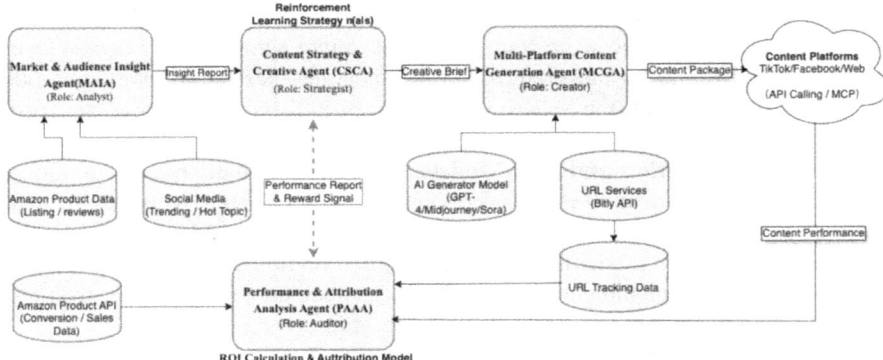

Fig. 1. Architecture of AI-Driven E-commerce Traffic Engine (AETE)

3. **Natural Language Processing and Analysis**: Applies a suite of Natural Language Processing (NLP) techniques to the collected corpus of user reviews. It uses topic modeling algorithms like BERTopic [5] to identify recurring themes. For comments within each theme, it performs Aspect-Based Sentiment Analysis (ABSA) [6, 7] to pinpoint specific features that users praise (e.g., "long battery life," "simple setup") and pain points they complain about (e.g., "unclear instructions," "bulky design").

4. **Output**: Generates a structured Insight Report containing:

   • A list of "Product Features & User Pain Points," ranked by sentiment polarity and frequency of mention.
   • A target audience profile based on social media trend analysis (e.g., "active on tech review YouTube channels," "follows specific lifestyle influencers on Instagram").

3.2   Content Strategy and Creative Agent (CSCA): the System's "Strategist"

• **Objective**: To select the optimal "content angle" and publishing platform to maximize expected ROI, based on current insights and historical performance.
• **Method**: This agent is implemented as a reinforcement learning (RL) agent.

   1. **State (s)**: The state space is defined by the Insight Report from MAIA and the historical performance data from PAAA. This gives the agent a comprehensive view of the "current market environment" and "past strategy effectiveness."
   2. **Action (a)**: The action space is designed as a discrete set of strategic "content angles" combined with target platforms. A "content angle" is an abstract creative direction, such as: {Angle: Address Pain Point B, Platform: YouTube}, {Angle: Showcase Feature A, Platform: Instagram}, {Angle: Lifestyle Integration, Platform: TikTok}, or {Angle: Unboxing Experience, Platform: YouTube}.
   3. **Policy ($\pi(a|s)$)**: The agent's policy, often implemented with a deep neural network like a Deep Q-Network (DQN) [9], estimates the long-term value (Q-value) of

each action a given the states. It then selects an action accordingly. In the initial phase, an ε-greedy strategy is used to balance exploration (trying new angles) and exploitation (choosing the known best angle).

4. **Output**: Generates a structured Creative Brief. This brief translates the chosen strategic action (content angle and platform) into specific, executable instructions for the next agent.

3.3 Multi-platform Content Generation Agent (MCGA): the System's "Creator"

- **Objective**: To produce and distribute high-quality, platform-native, multi-modal content according to the Creative Brief.
- **Process**:

   1. **Input**: Receives the Creative Brief from the CSCA.
   2. **Multi-modal Content Orchestration**: Acting as an orchestration layer, the MCGA calls upon multiple specialized generative models. It uses a large language model (e.g., GPT-4) [3] to write video scripts, post copy, or image captions based on the core message, tone, and target platform outlined in the brief. It then calls text-to-image or text-to-video models (e.g., Sora) [4] to generate visual assets that match the brief's stylistic requirements.
   3. **Affiliate Link Integration**: For each piece of content produced, the MCGA generates a unique tracking link for the target product via the Amazon Associates Program API [13]. It may also wrap this link using a URL shortening service (e.g., Bitly). This step is critical for enabling precise performance attribution.
   4. **Output**: Generates a "Content Package" containing the final video/image files, post text with relevant hashtags, and the embedded unique tracking link. The system can be configured to automatically publish the content via the respective platform APIs or submit it to a human review queue.

3.4 Performance and Attribution Analysis Agent (PAAA): the System's "Auditor"

- **Objective**: To accurately measure the real-world sales impact of each content instance and provide a quantitative reward for the CSCA's learning process.
- **Process:**

   1. **Data Collection**: Periodically pulls data via API from two sources: Amazon Affiliate reports (for clicks, conversions, and revenue generated through specific tracking IDs) [13] and the URL shortening service (for more granular click data).
   2. **Attribution**: Employs a direct attribution model [11]. Any sale completed via a specific tracking link is fully attributed to the content instance that published that link.
   3. **ROI Calculation and Reward Generation**: Calculates the return on investment (ROI) for each content instance. ROI is defined as:

$$ROI = \frac{(AttributedRevenue - EstimatedGenerationCost)}{EstimatedGenerationCost}$$

The generation cost can be estimated based on the API call fees and compute resources used for the models. The ROI from all instances under the same "content angle" is then aggregated to derive the average ROI for that strategy.

4. **Output**: Generates a Performance Report containing the reward (i.e., ROI) obtained for each action (content angle) taken. This report is fed back to the CSCA as the basis for updating its policy (e.g., updating its Q-value table) in its reinforcement learning algorithm.

4   Core Innovations

4.1   Semantic Analysis from Voice of Customer to Creative Strategy

AETE's primary innovation lies in the automated workflow from MAIA to CSCA, which systematically transforms a vast amount of unstructured user feedback and market trends into structured creative strategies ready for machine learning. By performing deep NLP analysis on hundreds or thousands of real user reviews, the system identifies the most resonant marketing messages directly from the "voice of the customer." The premise of this method—that online reviews contain signals of immense value to both consumers and businesses—is supported by existing research [12]. This mechanism ensures that the AI's creative strategy is not based on a generic list of features, but is rooted in empirical evidence of "what users truly care about," significantly enhancing the relevance and persuasive power of the content.

4.2   Reinforcement Learning Abstraction for Marketing Strategy

Our second key innovation is the design of the reinforcement learning framework within the CSCA [8]. Instead of having the RL agent decide on low-level tactical parameters like "which keyword to use" or "video length in seconds," we elevated its decision-making to the strategic level: choosing a "content angle." This abstraction offers two major advantages. First, it significantly reduces the action space, making the learning process more efficient and stable. Second, it enables the system to learn higher-level, more generalizable marketing strategies (e.g., "for product category X, focusing on solving user pain points is more profitable than simply showcasing features"). The learning process itself is one of exploring and discovering the optimal narrative patterns for different products and markets.

5   Proposed Experimental Validation

To validate the effectiveness and learning capability of AETE, we have designed a two-phase experiment conducted on a real Amazon product.

- **Preparation**: Select a product on Amazon that has a sufficient history of reviews (>50) and is eligible for the affiliate program (e.g., a mid-range consumer electronics item).
- **Experimental Phases**:

o **Phase 1: Baseline Establishment (2 weeks)**

B1 (Human Expert Baseline): An experienced marketing professional will manually create and publish social media content for the product based on their expert judgment, using a dedicated tracking link.

B2 (Non-learning System Baseline): A simplified version of AETE will be run where the CSCA is replaced by a random policy or a fixed heuristic based on MAIA's insights (e.g., "always choose the most frequently mentioned positive feature"). This baseline is intended to isolate and measure the value of the reinforcement learning component.

o **Phase 2: AETE Deployment & Learning (8 weeks)**: The full AETE system will be deployed. The RL agent in the CSCA will start with an exploratory policy (high ε-value) and will interact with users, collect feedback, and continuously update its strategy in the real environment.

- **Evaluation Metrics**:

  o **Primary Metric**: Total attributed revenue generated through affiliate links.
  o **Secondary Metrics**: Return on Investment (ROI) of the content, Click-Through Rate (CTR), and Conversion Rate (CVR).
  o **Process Metrics**: Track the frequency of the CSCA's selection of different "content angles" and the trend of the average ROI for these angles over time to visualize its learning process.

- **Hypotheses:**

  o **H1**: In the later stages of deployment (e.g., the final 4 weeks), the average daily attributed revenue generated by AETE will be significantly higher than that of the human expert baseline (B1).
  o **H2**: The total attributed revenue from AETE will be significantly higher than that from the non-learning system baseline (B2), demonstrating the effectiveness of the RL optimization component.
  o **H3**: During the AETE deployment period, the average ROI of the content angles selected by the system will show a statistically significant positive trend, indicating that its strategic learning is successful.

- **Appropriate statistical tests (e.g., t-tests)** will be used to verify the significance of the hypotheses.

6   Conclusion, Limitations, and Future Work

6.1   Conclusion

This paper has introduced the AETE, a novel solution designed to tackle the challenges of performance-driven e-commerce marketing in the real world. By framing the problem within a specialized multi-agent architecture [1, 2] and leveraging publicly available data sources and standard commercial APIs, AETE creates a fully closed-loop system capable of autonomous strategic planning, content creation, and iterative learning. Our proposed "user insight to creative brief" pipeline and the framework for optimizing "content angles" using reinforcement learning [8] are key contributions that advance the field from simple task automation toward intelligent, sales-focused strategy optimization. This research provides a concrete and viable blueprint for future autonomous marketing agents that can operate efficiently in the complex, uncontrolled environment of the open internet.

6.2 Limitations

While the AETE framework shows significant promise, we acknowledge several limitations. First, the system faces a "cold start" problem for newly launched products that lack a sufficient volume of user reviews. Second, its performance is heavily dependent on the reliability and data granularity of third-party APIs like the Amazon Associates Program [13]. Furthermore, the current direct attribution model [11] cannot capture the long-term effects of brand building or multiple content interactions on a final conversion. Finally, the ethical implications of AI generating marketing content at scale, such as the potential for manipulation or authenticity concerns, require further discussion and regulation.

6.3 Future Work

Future research can be pursued in several directions. First is the exploration of more sophisticated attribution models, potentially incorporating browsing data to build a more comprehensive view of the customer journey. Second, A/B testing mechanisms could be directly integrated into the CSCA's exploration process to more efficiently validate the effectiveness of content variations. Third, the system's capabilities could be expanded to manage paid advertising budgets, allowing for the co-optimization of content angle selection and ad placement strategy. Finally, we propose researching the integration of a "human-in-the-loop" mechanism, which would allow marketing experts to review and fine-tune the AI's strategies at critical decision points (e.g., before final content publication), thereby achieving an optimal synergy between human and machine intelligence.

References

1. Wooldridge, M.: An Introduction to MultiAgent Systems (2nd ed.). John Wiley & Sons (2009)
2. Dorri, A., Kanhere, S.S., Jurdak, R.: Multi-agent systems: a survey. IEEE Access **6**, 28573–28593 (2018)
3. OpenAI. GPT-4 Technical Report (2023). arXiv preprint arXiv:2303.08774
4. Brooks, T., Peebles, B., Holmes, C., DePue, W., Yu, W., Chen, J.: Video generation models as world simulators. OpenAI (2024)
5. Grootendorst, M.: BERTopic: Neural topic modeling with a class-based TF-IDF procedure (2022). arXiv preprint arXiv:2203.05794
6. Liu, B.: Sentiment analysis and opinion mining. Synth. Lect. Human Lang. Technol. **5**(1), 1–167 (2012)
7. Zhang, L., Wang, S., Liu, B.: Deep learning for sentiment analysis: a survey. Wiley Interdisc. Rev. Data Mining Knowl. Discov. **8**(4), e1253 (2018)

8. Sutton, R.S., Barto, A.G.: Reinforcement Learning: An Introduction. MIT Press (2018)
9. Mnih, V., et al.: Human-level control through deep reinforcement learning. Nature **518**(7540), 529–533 (2015)
10. Afsar, M.M., Crump, T., Far, B.: A review of reinforcement learning in e-commerce recommender systems. In: 2021 IEEE International Conference on Systems, Man, and Cybernetics (SMC) (pp. 1969–1976) (2021)
11. Li, H., Kannan, K.N.: Attributing conversions in a multichannel online marketing environment: an empirical model and a field experiment. J. Mark. Res. **51**(1), 40–56 (2014)
12. Chen, C.C., Tseng, Y.D.: Quality of online comments: a study of comment helpfulness from a consumer information processing perspective. J. Bus. Res. **64**(1), 23–30 (2011)
13. Amazon. (n.d.). Product Advertising API 5.0 Documentation. Amazon Associates Web Services. Retrieved July 19, 2025. https://webservices.amazon.com/paapi5/documentation/

Short Paper Track

Named Entity Recognition for Silk Road Trade Texts Based on Deep Learning

Boxuan Li, Qian Li[✉], and Yue Hu

School of Information Engineering, Minzu University of China, Beijing 100081, China
qianlimuc@muc.edu.cn

Abstract. With the proposal of the Belt and Road Initiative, research in the field of Silk Road trade has once again become a hotspot. This paper focuses on Named Entity Recognition (NER) for Silk Road Trade Texts Based on Deep Learning for Silk Road trade texts to support the knowledge graph development process. To address the absence of standardized datasets and noise interference in Silk Road trade research, we construct an annotated corpus by aggregating multi-source raw data, deploying DeepSeek-R1's domain adaptation for noise filtering, followed by LangChain-based paragraph-level semantic segmentation to support NER training. Subsequently, it proposes an innovative deep learning model named BERT-BiGRU-Attention-CRF for entity recognition in Silk Road trade texts. This model synergistically combines BERT's deep semantic understanding, BiGRU's capability for modeling long-range dependencies, the attention mechanism's focus on critical information, and CRF's optimization of label sequence constraints. Results from comparative experiments with other entity recognition models illustrate that our proposed model exhibits better performance and higher accuracy. It effectively addresses the key challenge of entity recognition posed by long-range dependencies and complex contextual semantics inherent in Silk Road trade texts, thereby laying a solid foundation for constructing high-quality Silk Road trade knowledge graphs.

Keywords: Silk Road trade · deep learning · named entity recognition · BERT-BIGRU-Attention-CRF · knowledge graph

1 Introduction

The Silk Road, a vital conduit for cultural and economic exchange between ancient Eastern and Western civilizations, has exerted profound influences on global economic development [1]. With the proposal of the Belt and Road Initiative [2], scholarly interest in Silk Road studies, particularly trade-related research, has resurged significantly. However, conventional research methodologies struggle to analyze massive-scale data effectively and unveil intrinsic patterns underlying Silk Road trade. The advent of deep learning techniques has opened new avenues for Silk Road trade studies [3]. Deep learning models can effectively handle massive volumes of data and extract key features from complex information, thereby enabling comprehensive and in-depth insights into

Y. Yang et al. (Eds.): ICCC 2025, LNCS 16156, pp. 77–85, 2026.
https://doi.org/10.1007/978-3-032-06310-6_6

historical trade dynamics. Building upon this foundation, knowledge graph construction further enhances analytical capabilities [4–6]. As a structured semantic network, knowledge graphs transform fragmented data into an inferential and interconnected knowledge system through entity-relation-attribute triples. While knowledge graphs provide a structural framework for integrating historical knowledge fragments, their construction critically depends on the accuracy of named entity recognition (NER) [7–9]. Existing deep learning models face notable challenges in recognizing Silk Road trade entities due to long-distance dependencies, semantic ambiguities, and sparse annotations in historical texts. This study focuses on developing a high-precision NER model tailored for constructing a Silk Road trade knowledge graph.

Named Entity Recognition (NER), a core NLP task and vital component for knowledge graph construction, detects and classifies entities (e.g., persons, locations, organizations, events) in unstructured text [10]. Recent deep learning advancements reveal two trends: enhanced contextual encoding and optimized sequence modeling. While Chiu et al.'s LSTM-CRF model performs well on standard datasets [11], its short-range dependency modeling fails to capture cross-span entity associations in Silk Road trade texts. Subramanian et al.'s BERT approach [12] improves accuracy but struggles with transliterated term ambiguities due to static encoding. Subsequent models like BERT-BiLSTM-CRF [13] reduce manual dependency yet suffer from BiLSTM's gradient decay in long-entity boundary recognition. Though BERT-CA-BiLSTM [14] and RoBERTa-BiLSTM-CRF [15] boost performance via pretraining or attention mechanisms, they inadequately address coupled challenges of long-range dependencies and contextual complexity. Chen et al.'s BiGRU-based stacked attention network [16] achieves efficient global feature extraction in biomedical NER but lacks domain adaptation. Similarly, Cheng et al.'s MacBERT-BiGRU-Attention model [17] balances complexity and performance but remains limited in Silk Road-specific scenarios like transliterations due to domain-agnostic design.

Addressing these gaps, we propose the BERT-BiGRU-Attention-CRF framework to tackle long-range dependencies and contextual intricacies (e.g., transliterated terms, historical-modern entity aliases) in Silk Road trade texts. Evaluated on our purpose-built dataset, the model demonstrates significant improvements in entity recognition.

2 Methodology

This paper proposes a BERT-BiGRU-Attention-CRF deep learning model for end-to-end named entity recognition. The framework synergistically addresses core challenges in Silk Road trade texts through four integrated components: The BERT layer employs domain-adaptive pretraining on specialized corpora to resolve transliteration ambiguities; the BiGRU layer captures long-range entity dependencies via gated state persistence, overcoming BiLSTM's gradient decay limitations; attention mechanisms dynamically suppress contextual noise from non-entity descriptors; while the CRF layer enforces consistent entity boundary labeling through constrained transition rules. The input text is first transformed into context-aware embeddings by the BERT layer, then processed by the BiGRU layer to capture sequential temporal patterns. The BiGRU outputs are refined through multi-head attention for contextual enhancement, and finally decoded by the

CRF layer with global sequence optimization. All layers are jointly trained via back-propagation, integrating BERT's semantic comprehension, BiGRU's sequential modeling, attention-based focus, and CRF's structural decoding to generate grammatically and domain-constrained entity labels, as illustrated in Fig. 1.

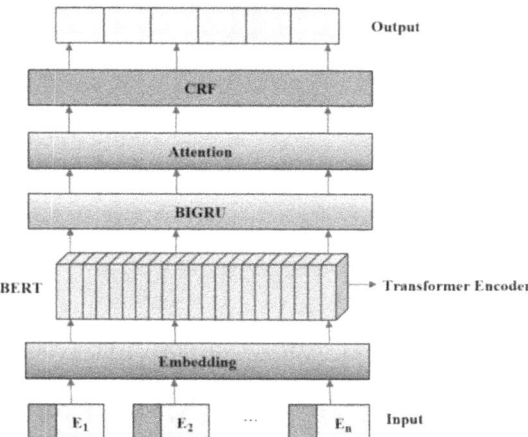

Fig. 1. Architecture of BERT-BIGRU-Attention-CRF.

2.1 BERT

BERT, a Transformer-based pretrained language model, uses bidirectional training to generate context-aware embeddings. This enables better semantic understanding across contexts through Masked Language Modeling and Next Sentence Prediction objectives. The BERT architecture is illustrated in Fig. 2.

The core of BERT lies in its Transformer encoder, which employs a self-attention mechanism to capture dependency relationships between words in text. This self-attention mechanism enables the model to simultaneously consider all other words in the input sequence when processing each token, thereby establishing global contextual understanding. Each Transformer encoder layer comprises two key components:

$$\text{Attention}(Q, K, V) = \text{softmax}\left(\frac{QK^T}{\sqrt{d_k}}\right)V \tag{1}$$

$$\text{MultiHead}(X) = [\text{head}_1; ...; \text{head}_h]W^O \tag{2}$$

$$\text{Head}_i = \text{Attention}\left(XW_i^Q, XW_i^K, XW_i^V\right) \tag{3}$$

where $\mathbf{W_i^Q}, \mathbf{W_i^K}, \mathbf{W_i^V} \in \mathbf{R^{d \times dk}}$ represents projection matrices for queries, keys and values, then h represents number of attention heads, and $\mathbf{d_k = d/h}$ represents dimension

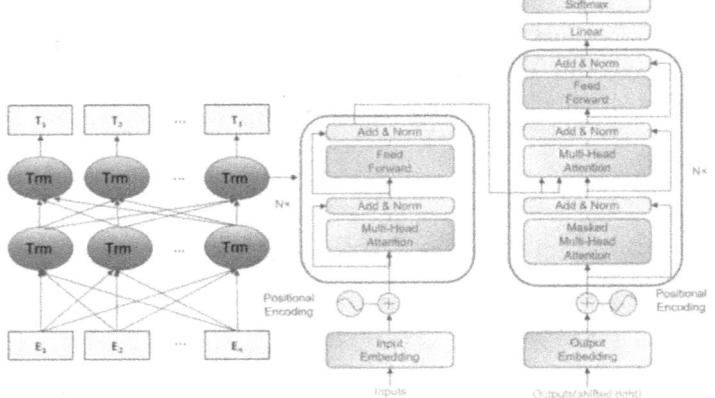

Fig. 2. Architecture of BERT.

of each head. The final output of the BERT model is the context-dependent vector representations processed by multiple Transformer encoder layers.

In our model, the output vectors from BERT serve as input to the BiGRU layer. Specifically, for each position i in the input sequence, the corresponding BERT output vector is fed into the subsequent BiGRU network for further processing.

2.2 BiGRU

BiGRU combines bidirectional temporal modeling to capture dependencies in BERT embeddings, enhancing long-range boundary detection for Silk Road texts. Its GRU core merges LSTM's input/forget gates into an update gate with reset gate, resolving RNN gradient issues via streamlined gating. This dual-gate design is more efficient than triple-gate BiLSTM. The BiGRU framework is illustrated in Fig. 3.

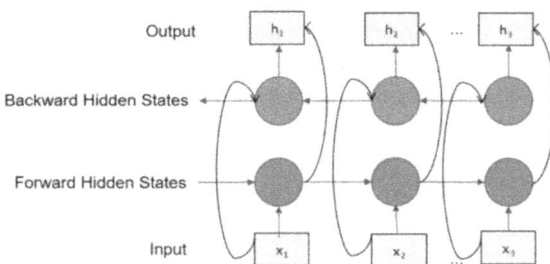

Fig. 3. Architecture of BIGRU.

Assume that $\mathbf{x_t}$ is the input vector at time step $\mathbf{t}$. The computational process of the GRU network is expressed as follows:

$$z_t = \sigma(W_z x_t + U_z h_{t-1} + b_z) \tag{4}$$

$$r_t = \sigma(W_r x_t + U_r h_{t-1} + b_r) \tag{5}$$

$$\underset{t}{\underline{h}} = \tanh(W_h x_t + U_h(r_t \times h_t - 1) + b_h) \tag{6}$$

$$\underset{t}{\underline{h}} = z_t \times h_{t-1} + (1 - z_t) \times \underset{t}{\underline{h}} \tag{7}$$

where z_t and r_t represent the update gate and reset gate, respectively, $\underline{h}_t$ represents the candidate hidden state, h_{t-1} and h_t represent the hidden states at time steps $t - 1$ and t, W and U are weight matrices, b is the bias term, σ denotes the sigmoid function. The output of BiGRU consists of hidden state sequences that incorporate bidirectional temporal features:

$$H^{gru} = [h_1, h_2, ..., h_n] \in R^{n \times 2h} \tag{8}$$

2.3 Attention

The attention mechanism provides context-sensitive feature enhancement by dynamically evaluating semantic relevance between words. In this study, the mechanism addresses the long-distance dependency problem between modifiers and entities in Silk Road texts. It captures semantic association across dimensions through multi-head computation and assigns higher weights to key contexts. The output of attention-weighted vectors emphasizes context features related to entities, stamps out noise, and enhances recognition accuracy of complex entity boundaries.

2.4 CRF

The CRF layer ensures global sequence coherence by modeling label transition constraints. It decodes attention-layer vectors using a transition matrix to prevent illegal label combinations, incorporating current token probabilities and adjacent-label transitions to determine the optimal sequence via the Viterbi algorithm:

$$P(y|x) \propto \exp\left(\sum_t (W h_t + A_{yt-1,yt})\right) \tag{9}$$

where W represents the emission weight matrix and A represents the label transition matrix. This mechanism enhances entity boundary detection accuracy, especially for long and nested entities, ensuring label consistency. The CRF layer outperforms plain Softmax classification in NER tasks.

3 Experiments

3.1 Data Sources and Preprocessing

Due to the absence of public datasets for Silk Road trade research, this work constructs a dedicated corpus by aggregating raw textual data from dispersed sources including encyclopedias and Belt and Road Initiative portals. Some of the data is shown in Fig. 4. To address noise interference in raw data and facilitate efficient NER model training, we develop a hybrid text optimization pipeline integrating LangChain and DeepSeek-R1. This framework converts complex unstructured texts into standardized shallow semantic representations through DeepSeek-R1's domain-adaptive noise filtering followed by LangChain's paragraph-level semantic segmentation, ensuring semantic integrity for downstream processing units.

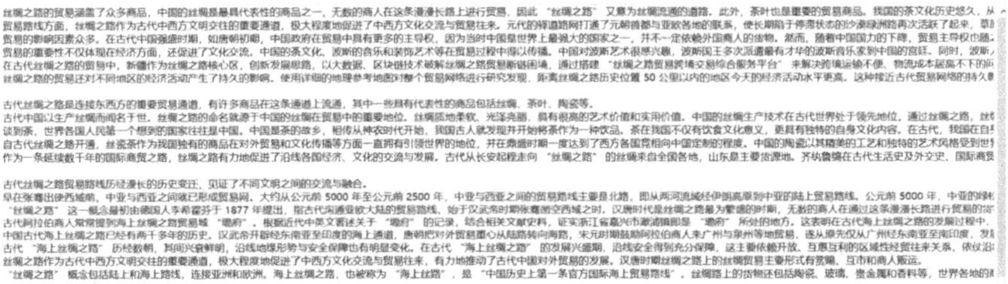

Fig. 4. Some data on Silk Road trade.

3.2 Data Annotation

Part-of-speech tagging refers to the procedure of giving syntactic category labels to each word or lexical entity in text, which facilitates more precise computational linguistic analysis and procedure. In this study, we performed data annotation on approximately 2,000 preprocessed short sentences using Label Studio. Annotation guidelines were established following the BIO (Begin-Inside-Outside) tagging scheme, with the formatted outputs structured into dataset for NER tasks. Some sentences of the Silk Road trade entity dataset obtained by processing a sample sentence in BIO format are illustrated in Fig. 5. The entity categories annotated and their quantitative distribution are illustrated in Table 1.

```
{"text": ["栗", "特", "商", "人", "酿", "造", "芳", "香", "葡", "萄", "酒"], "labels": ["B-PERSON", "I-PERSON", "I-PERSON", "I-PERSON", "O", "O",
"B-PRODUCT", "I-PRODUCT", "I-PRODUCT", "I-PRODUCT", "I-PRODUCT"]}
{"text": ["张", "骞", "与", "大", "月", "氏", "王", "签", "约", "了", "互", "通", "有", "无", "的", "协", "定"], "labels": ["B-PERSON", "I-PERSON", "O",
"B-PERSON", "I-PERSON", "I-PERSON", "I-PERSON", "O", "O", "O", "B-TRADE", "I-TRADE", "I-TRADE", "I-TRADE", "I-TRADE", "I-TRADE",
"I-TRADE"]}
{"text": ["张", "骞", "出", "使", "西", "域", "推", "动", "了", "丝", "路", "早", "期", "的", "开", "拓"], "labels": ["B-PERSON", "I-PERSON", "O", "O",
"B-LOCATION", "I-LOCATION", "O", "O", "O", "B-EVENT", "I-EVENT", "I-EVENT", "I-EVENT", "I-EVENT", "I-EVENT", "I-EVENT"]}
{"text": ["玄", "奘", "与", "天", "竺", "国", "王", "订", "立", "了", "经", "书", "交", "换", "协", "定"], "labels": ["B-PERSON", "I-PERSON", "O", "O",
"O", "O", "O", "O", "B-TRADE", "I-TRADE", "I-TRADE", "I-TRADE", "I-TRADE", "I-TRADE"]}
```

Fig. 5. Silk Road Trade Entity Dataset Sentences Examples.

Table 1. Entity categories and quantities.

Entity category	quantity
Person	407
Route	66
Construct	82
Organization	83
Policy	105
Event	83
Period	95
Culture	97
Commodity	186
Location	176

3.3 Named Entity Recognition

For the NER task, the dataset was randomly split into training and evaluation sets, utilizing 85% and 15% of the entity data, respectively. To validate the effectiveness of the proposed entity recognition model, comparative experiments were conducted against multiple classic deep learning models. Precision, Recall, and F1-score were adopted as assessment metrics. The experimental results are illustrated in Table 2.

Table 2. Comparison of Entity Recognition Model Results.

Model	Precision	Recall	F1
CRF	50.7634	44.9324	58.3333
BILSTM-CRF	73.0361	70.7819	75.4386
BIGRU-CRF	73.1092	70.1613	76.3158
BERT-Softmax	85.4664	84.5494	86.4035
BERT-BILSTM-Softmax	86.2745	85.7143	86.8421
BERT-BIGRU-Softmax	86.5542	85.8617	86.9369
BERT-CRF	87.0897	86.8996	87.0811
BERT-BILSTM-CRF	87.4725	87.6652	87.2807
BERT-BIGRU-CRF	87.6652	88.0531	87.2807
BERT-BILSTM-Attention-CRF	88.1057	88.2096	87.7193
BERT-BIGRU-Attention-CRF(ours)	**88.4026**	**88.4996**	**88.5965**

Experimental results show that the BERT-BiGRU-Attention-CRF model achieves optimal performance. The balanced precision and recall metrics indicate that the attention layer effectively amplifies the semantic weighting of critical modifiers, while the BiGRU architecture ensures computational efficiency without sacrificing model simplicity. Notably, in long-entity recognition tasks, this model outperforms the baseline BERT-CRF by a 1.52 F1-score improvement. The proposed architecture provides a reliable entity annotation foundation for subsequent knowledge graph construction.

4   Conclusion

This study presents a deep learning model for named entity recognition applied to multi-source Silk Road trade texts. The BERT-BiGRU-Attention-CRF framework addresses entity representation challenges through BERT's domain-adaptive pre-training, captures cross-sentence dependencies via BiGRU's bidirectional temporal modeling, enhances semantic weighting with attention mechanisms, and ensures global sequence validity via CRF's label transition constraints. Experimental results demonstrate the model's superior recognition performance. The constructed knowledge graph establishes a structured data foundation for Belt and Road and Digital Silk Road research, enabling trade visualization. Future work will implement relation extraction and knowledge storage to advance digital Silk Road trade studies.

References

1. Chen, Y., Luo, P., Chang, T.: Economic nexus among the belt and road initiative participating countries. North Am. J. Econ. Finance **77**, 102403 (2025)
2. Baniya, S., Rocha, N., Ruta, M.: Trade effects of the new silk road: a gravity analysis. J. Dev. Econ. **146**, 102467 (2020)
3. Li, H., Shen, J., Song, W.: Research on the belt and road international network optimization initiative based on deep learning. Front. Traffic Transp. Eng. **4**(1) (2024)
4. Choi, S., Jung, Y.: Knowledge graph construction: extraction, learning, and evaluation. Appl. Sci. **15**(7), 3727 (2025)
5. Payal, C., Kexin, H., Marinka, Z.: Building a knowledge graph to enable precision medicine. Sci. Data **10**(1), 67 (2023)
6. Cai, K., Chen, Z., Li, J., et al.: Construction of earth observation knowledge hub based on knowledge graph. Trans. GIS **28**(7), 2445–2462 (2024)
7. Lagutina, S.N., Vasilyev, M.A., Zafievsky, D.D.: Tasks in named entity recognition: technologies and tools. Autom. Control. Comput. Sci. **58**(7), 779–796 (2025)
8. Kumar, M., Singh, P., Kashtriya, P.: Enhanced biomedical named entity recognition using SpaCy and BERT models. Procedia Comput. Sci. **258**, 1954–1961 (2025)
9. Ke, X., Wu, X., Ou, Z., et al.: Chinese Named Entity Recognition method based on multi-feature fusion and biaffine. Complex Intell. Syst. **10**(5), 6305–6318 (2024)
10. Huang, W., Yu, X.: Named entity recognition method based on multi-feature fusion. Appl. Sci. **15**(1), 388 (2025)
11. Chiu, J.P.C., Nichols, E.: Named entity recognition with bidirectional LSTM-CNNs. Trans. Assoc. Comput. Linguist. **4**, 357–370 (2015)

12. Lample, G., Ballesteros, M., Subramanian, S., et al.: Neural architectures for named entity recognition. In: Proceedings of the 2016 Conference of the North American Chapter of the Association for Computational Linguistics: Human Language Technologies, pp. 260–270 (2016)
13. Li, Y., Luo, L., Zeng, X., et al.: Fine-tuned BERT-BiLSTM-CRF approach for named entity recognition in geological disaster texts. Earth Sci. Inf. **18**(2), 368 (2025)
14. Huang, Q., Tao, Y., Wu, Z., et al.: Based on BERT-wwm for agricultural named entity recognition. Agronomy **14**(6), 1217 (2024)
15. Li, B., Cheng, H., Lin, M.: SESG-optimizing information extraction in Chinese clinical texts: an innovative named entity recognition approach using RoBERTa-BiLSTM-CRF mechanism. J. Inform. Knowl. Manag. **23**(06) (2024)
16. JieQing, C., ZhiChao, Z., Feng, Z., et al.: A BIGRU-based stacked attention network for biomedical named entity recognition with Chinese EMRs. Stud. Health Technol. Inform. **308**, 757–767 (2023)
17. Yuan, C., Tang, F., Shan, C., et al.: Exploring named entity recognition via MacBERT-BiGRU and global pointer with self-attention. Big Data Cogn. Comput. **8**(12), 179 (2024)

MusicNER: With Adversarial Training and Attention Mechanisms for Chinese Musical Instrument NER

Yina Zhang, Qian Li[✉], and Jiayuan Wang

School of Information Engineering, Minzu University of China, Beijing 100081, China
qianlimuc@muc.edu.cn

Abstract. Named Entity Recognition (NER) in texts about Chinese traditional musical instruments faces challenges due to composite structures that blur entity boundaries and difficulties like dialect transliterations. To address these issues, this paper proposes a novel NER model that integrates adversarial training and a cross-attention mechanism. During the fine-tuning stage of Bidirectional Encoder Representations from Transformers (BERT) word embeddings, the model introduces adversarial training. It enhances the model's ability to learn robust features by applying perturbations. Next, the model constructs a parallel feature extraction network comprising Iterated Dilated Convolutional Neural Network (IDCNN) and Bidirectional Gated Recurrent Unit (BiGRU). It also designs a cross-attention fusion module. This module enables the dynamic weighted fusion of context-aware features. Finally, the model employs a Conditional Random Field (CRF) decoder to constrain label transition logic. Experiments conducted on our self-built Chinese musical instrument text dataset show that the proposed model achieves an F_1 score of 83.27%. This performance outperforms baseline models.

Keywords: Named Entity Recognition · Chinese Musical Instruments · Adversarial Training

1 Introduction

Named Entity Recognition (NER) [1] is a fundamental task in Natural Language Processing (NLP). It identifies named entities like person names, locations, and organizations in textual corpora. NER enables critical applications including information extraction, knowledge graph construction, and machine translation. With advancing cultural digitization, deep information mining and knowledge organization of Chinese traditional musical instrument texts have become essential. Effective NER techniques extract key information from these texts, providing strong support for preserving and inheriting Chinese musical instrument culture. However, NER for Chinese musical instrument texts faces unique challenges. These texts contain diverse entity categories with specialized terminology. Such terms carry specific cultural connotations and differ significantly from general-domain vocabulary, increasing recognition difficulty.

Y. Yang et al. (Eds.): ICCC 2025, LNCS 16156, pp. 86–94, 2026.
https://doi.org/10.1007/978-3-032-06310-6_7

Traditional NER approaches exhibit limitations: Rule-based methods rely on manually crafted rules. For complex musical instrument texts, rule formulation proves difficult and fails to cover all cases. Statistical machine learning methods automatically learn textual features but perform poorly on long-distance dependencies and complex semantics. Recent deep learning advances have significantly improved NER. Pre-trained language models like BERT [2] learn rich linguistic knowledge through large-scale corpus pre-training. Nevertheless, these methods remain inadequate for musical instrument texts.

To overcome these limitations, we propose a novel NER model integrating adversarial training and cross-attention. Our design includes: (1) Adversarial training during word embedding optimization, adding perturbations to learn robust features against labeling noise. (2)Parallel BiGRU-IDCNN architecture leveraging BiGRU's long-range dependency capture and IDCNN's local feature extraction. (3)Cross-attention mechanism enabling inter-layer feature interaction to enhance representation capability.

2 Related Work

The Named Entity Recognition (NER) task extracts structured information from unstructured text. This information supports various applications like sentiment analysis, knowledge graph construction [3], and machine translation. NER methodology has evolved through three stages: rule-based, machine learning-based, and deep learning-based approaches. Rule-based methods achieve higher recall and precision on smaller-scale data. These approaches rely on linguistic knowledge and expert experience to identify entities via constructed rules and dictionaries [4]. Kim et al. proposed rule induction using part-of-speech tags. While adaptable to specific domains, these methods struggle to cover all linguistic phenomena. Rule creation is labor-intensive, and systems exhibit poor portability.

Machine learning-based methods automatically learn entity features and patterns from annotated data without manual rule definition. They offer greater adaptability and flexibility. Primary supervised models include Hidden Markov Models (HMM), Maximum Entropy Models (MEM), Support Vector Machines (SVM), and Conditional Random Fields (CRF). Shuang et al. [5] enhanced HMM with backward feature representations. This captures contextual information to improve extraction quality. Unlike rule-based approaches, these methods transform NER into sequence labeling. They eliminate manual lexicons and extend applicability to unseen samples. However, limitations persist: Feature selection critically impacts performance, effectiveness depends heavily on training corpora, building high-quality datasets requires substantial investment, and models exhibit weak generalization.

Deep learning-based methods surpass rule-based and statistical approaches by requiring less manual feature engineering, demonstrating stronger learning capacity, and achieving better performance on smaller corpora. Liu et al. [6] proposed a BiLSTM-CRF baseline. They improved accuracy and recall using domain-adaptive embeddings from concatenated character and pretrained vectors, achieving state-of-the-art (SOTA) performance. Huang et al. [7] used Artificial Neural Networks (ANN) for expressive word vectors. They extracted local features via CNN and fed these to BiLSTM to enhance text representation learning. These studies highlight deep learning's cross-domain applicability. Zhang et al. [8] proposed a novel global word boundary detection method. It employs a self-attention mechanism to capture semantic dependencies. This approach assigns compatibility weights to each character in sentences, representing character embeddings.

To further enhance the quality and expressiveness of word vectors, static language models were integrated into the embedding layer. Zhu et al. [9] employed the GloVe model to generate an embedding lookup table, converting word sequences into low-dimensional vectors for deep learning model input. Yun et al. [10] addressed NER tasks in the music domain using a BLSTM-CRF baseline model with BERT-trained Chinese character vectors, achieving a 9.89% improvement over baseline results. Yang et al. [11] optimized semantic representations for geological texts by extracting finer-grained features, constructing a BERT-BiLSTM-IDCNN-CRF framework for precise lithium deposit entity extraction that attained an 88% F_1 score. Rui et al. [12] utilized the MERNIE pre-trained model for corpus vectorization, significantly improving recognition of polysemous words and musical terminology in intangible cultural heritage domains. Pan et al. [13] enhanced entity label generation accuracy through adversarial training on low-resource datasets, reaching an 86.86% F_1 score on their self-built dataset.

3 MusicNER Model

In this paper, we propose a Named Entity Recognition (NER) model for Chinese musical instrument texts, which integrates adversarial training and a cross-attention mechanism. We refer to this model as MusicNER (Fig. 1).

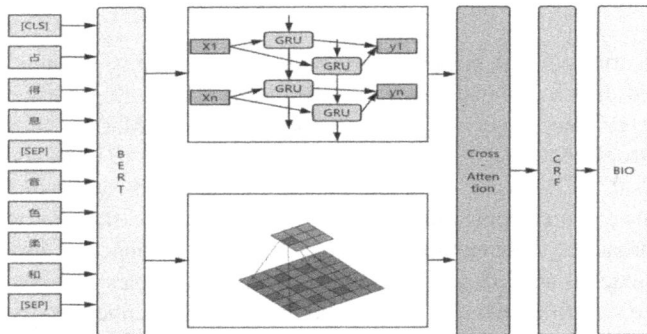

Fig. 1. The architecture of MusicNER comprises four modules: the BERT pre-trained encoder, the parallel multi-scale feature extractor, the bidirectional cross-attention fusion layer, and the CRF sequence decoding layer.

3.1 BERT Encoding and Adversarial Training Enhancement

BERT Model. Our model employs the pre-trained language model BERT as the foundational encoder. Its innovation lies in the bidirectional encoding mechanism and large-scale pre-training approach. This enables BERT to learn deep semantic information within text. The bidirectional encoding considers both left and right context of the input simultaneously. This capability captures richer semantic information, leading to more accurate understanding of sentence meaning.

Like most deep learning models for NLP, BERT sends each token to the token embedding layer for vector representation. However, BERT uniquely incorporates two additional embedding layers: segment embeddings and position embeddings. These three embeddings (Token, Position, Segment) serve distinct functions that collectively enhance BERT's understanding of text semantics, structure, and sequence. Token Embedding comprehends vocabulary semantics, Position Embedding provides positional information, and Segment Embedding distinguishes inter-sentence relationships. Through this combined embedding scheme, BERT demonstrates powerful contextual understanding across NLP tasks (Fig. 2).

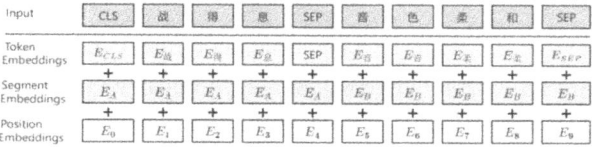

Fig. 2. Example Diagram of BERT Input.

Adversarial Training. To enhance model robustness against input perturbations and improve generalization capability for Named Entity Recognition (NER) in complex linguistic environments, this paper introduces a Fast Gradient Method (FGM)-based adversarial training strategy during model training. This method adds targeted minor perturbations to the word embedding layer, forcing the model to learn simultaneously from original samples and their adversarially perturbed versions. This effectively strengthens resistance to input disturbances. The adversarial perturbation vector calculation is given in Eq. 1.

$$x_{adv} = x + \frac{\nabla_x \ell(\theta, x, y)}{\|\nabla \ell(\theta, x, y)\|_2} \tag{1}$$

In actual training, our adversarial training mechanism embeds within each training step through three phases: (a) Standard forward and backward propagation: First perform a forward pass with original samples, calculate loss and execute a backward pass to obtain the loss gradient with respect to input embeddings. (b) Adversarial perturbation construction and propagation: After obtaining gradients, construct perturbations using Eq. 1, add them to original embeddings to generate adversarial examples, perform another forward pass to compute adversarial loss, then execute backward propagation to accumulate adversarial gradients. (c) Gradient update and embedding restoration:

Following both backward passes, merge gradients from original and adversarial samples, update parameters via optimizer, then restore embeddings to pre-perturbation state ensuring perturbations don't permanently affect embedding representations.

3.2 Enhancement Feature Extraction

Based on the output of BERT, we construct a parallel feature extraction structure that combines BiGRU and a IDCNN. Although BERT provides certain contextual modeling capabilities, introducing task-specific shallow encoders helps better capture position-sensitive and local structural features. The BiGRU module is mainly used to model long-range dependencies in the input sequence. The calculation procedure is shown in Eqs. 2 to 4.

$$h_t{}^{\rightarrow} = GRU(x_t, \overrightarrow{h_{t-1}}) \tag{2}$$

$$h_t{}^{\leftarrow} = GRU(x_t, \overleftarrow{h_{t-1}}) \tag{3}$$

$$h_t = [\overrightarrow{h_t} \oplus \overleftarrow{h_t}] \tag{4}$$

The final output of BiGRU is the concatenation of the two directions: The input x_t at the present time, the forward hidden layer output $\overrightarrow{h_{t-1}}$, and the reverse hidden layer output $\overleftarrow{h_{t-1}}$ at the prior time determine the present time hidden layer output state ht of BiGRU.

To fully integrate information from BiGRU and IDCNN streams, this paper introduces a cross-attention mechanism for selective alignment and interaction across distinct feature spaces. This mechanism simulates inter-stream information-attention relationships, enabling dynamic focus on the most discriminative feature regions. The fused features are provided in Eq. 5.

$$H_{fused} = CrossAtten(G, C) \oplus CrossAtten(C, G) \tag{5}$$

3.3 Model Decoding

This paper introduces a CRF decoding layer after the feature extraction module to better model dependencies between labels. In Named Entity Recognition (NER), structural constraints between labels are evident – for example, in the BIO scheme, an "I-Person" tag should not follow a "B-Instrument" tag.

4 Experiments

Research in musical instrument domains—such as instrument recognition, timbre classification, music generation, and recommendation—typically relies on large-scale, high-quality datasets. However, datasets in this field remain scarce. This paper constructs a Chinese musical instrument text dataset sourced from Baidu Baike and Musical Instruments of Chinese Ethnic Minorities (Fig. 3).

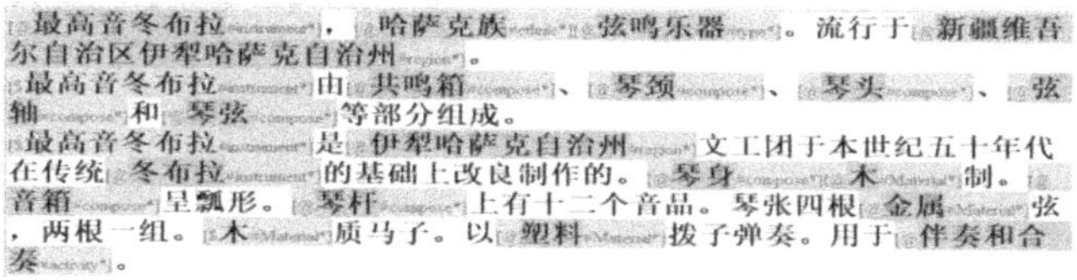

最高音冬布拉，哈萨克族弦鸣乐器。流行于新疆维吾尔自治区伊犁哈萨克自治州。最高音冬布拉由共鸣箱、琴颈、琴头、弦轴和琴弦等部分组成。最高音冬布拉是伊犁哈萨克自治州文工团于本世纪五十年代在传统冬布拉的基础上改良制作的。琴身木制。音箱呈瓢形。琴杆上有十二个音品。琴张四根金属弦，两根一组。木质马子。以塑料拨子弹奏。用于伴奏和合奏。

Fig. 3. Musical Instrument Text Examples.

Table 1. Details of the datasets.

Entity type	Example	Number of entities
Instrument	最高音冬布拉	2470
Preson	李鸣	186
Work	乌拉调	519
Activity	婚丧嫁娶	631
Material	桐木	1732
Region	广西壮族自治区	1271
Type	膜鸣乐器	412
Ethnic	汉族	1019
Timbre	明亮	570
Compose	琴头	1558

The specific entity categories in the dataset are listed in the Table 1.

To comprehensively evaluate the model's performance on the Named Entity Recognition (NER) task, this paper employs three core metrics commonly used in Natural Language Processing (NLP): Precision, Recall, and F_1 score. The calculation formulas are as follows Eqs. 6 to 8.

$$P = \frac{T_P}{T_P + F_P} * 100\% \tag{6}$$

$$R = \frac{T_P}{T_P + F_N} * 100\% \tag{7}$$

$$F_1 = \frac{2PR}{P + R} * 100\% \tag{8}$$

All experiments in this study were conducted in the Python 3.6.7 programming environment. We implemented the models using the PyTorch 2.1.0 deep learning framework. To accelerate the computation, we performed model training and testing on an NVIDIA GeForce RTX 4090 GPU. This GPU provides 24GB of dedicated memory. The hyperparameters are detailed in Table 2.

As shown in the Table 3, the traditional BiLSTM-CRF model performs weakest with an F1 score of 75.36%, indicating that conventional sequence modeling alone inadequately extracts deep semantic features. The standalone CRF slightly outperforms BiLSTM-CRF, suggesting that structurally simple decoders with global optimization capabilities still contribute meaningfully. After introducing the pre-trained BERT model, performance improves significantly: BERT-CRF achieves an F1 score of 81.50%, demonstrating BERT's superior contextual semantic encoding. Further combining BERT with BiGRU or IDCNN followed by a CRF layer yields continuous gains, where BERT-BiGRU-CRF and BERT-IDCNN-CRF reach 81.96% and 81.67% respectively, validating sequence modules' efficacy in extracting local contextual features.

Table 2. Name of parameter and Value of a parameter.

Name of parameter	Value of a parameter
BERT embedding dim	768
Batch size	16
Learning rate	6e-5
Dropout rate	0.1
Optimizer	Adam
BiGRU hidden unit size	128
Epoth	50

To better integrate diverse feature extraction structures, we construct the BERT-IDCNN-BiGRU-CRF model. Its parallel multi-dimensional feature extraction achieves balanced contextual modeling, raising the F_1 score to 81.98%. Subsequent integration of adversarial training enhances robustness. The BERT-FGM-IDCNN-BiGRU-CRF model improves all metrics, attaining a 82.27% F_1 score. This confirms adversarial perturbations effectively increase error tolerance for noisy samples.Finally, incorporating the cross-attention mechanism into this architecture yields the proposed MusicNER model. It achieves optimal results across all metrics with an F_1 score of 83.27%—a 1.77 percentage point improvement over the baseline BERT-CRF model. This demonstrates the cross-attention mechanism's effectiveness in feature fusion. Our model achieves F_1 scores of 96.2% on Timbre and 74.33% on Instrument, surpassing all baseline models.

Table 3. Results from various models applied to our datasets.

Model	P	R	F_1
CRF	81.70	72.99	76.86
BiLSTM-CRF	76.85	73.92	75.36
BERT-CRF	80.40	82.64	81.50
BERT-BiGRU-CRF	80.33	83.66	81.96
BERT-IDCNN-CRF	81.47	81.88	81.67

(*continued*)

Table 3. (*continued*)

Model	P	R	F_1
BERT-IDCNNBiGRU-CRF	81.98	82.69	81.98
BERT-FGM-IDCNNBiGRU-CRF	81.65	82.90	82.27
MusicNER	82.48	84.08	83.27

5 Conclusion

This study proposes a multi-feature fusion model integrating adversarial training and cross-attention for NER in Chinese traditional musical instruments. Building upon the BERT, the architecture incorporates parallel BiGRU and IDCNN structures to extract contextual semantic features and local structural patterns. This effectively compensates for single-structure modeling limitations. We design a cross-attention mechanism establishing inter-representation associations between BiGRU and IDCNN outputs, enhancing semantic expressiveness. To strengthen robustness and generalization, adversarial training perturbs embeddings during backpropagation. This significantly improves performance on few-shot and long-tail categories without increasing inference overhead. During decoding, a CRF layer models entity label transitions. Experiments on our constructed Chinese musical instrument knowledge graph dataset validate the model's effectiveness. Results demonstrate superiority over strong baselines across metrics, achieving an 83.27% F_1 score.

Future work includes: (1) Implementing advanced global attention to strengthen entity relationship modeling (2) Expanding datasets to explore few-shot learning and transfer learning for specialized domain NER.

References

1. Diefenbach, D., Lopez, V., Singh, K., et al.: Core techniques of question answering systems over knowledge bases: a survey. Knowl. Inf. Syst. **55**(3), 529–569 (2018)
2. Souza, F., Nogueira, R., Lotufo, R.: Portuguese named entity recognition using BERT-CRF. arXiv preprint arXiv:1909.10649 (2019)
3. Peng, C., Xia, F., Naseriparsa, M., et al.: Knowledge graphs: opportunities and challenges. Artif. Intell. Rev. **56**(11), 13071–13102 (2023)
4. Wang, Y., Tong, H., Zhu, Z., et al.: Nested named entity recognition: a survey. ACM Trans. Knowl. Discovery Data (TKDD) **16**(6), 1–29 (2022)
5. Shuang, Z., et al.: Research and application for web information extraction based on improved hidden Markov model. Comput. Appl. Softw. **34**, 42–47 (2017)
6. Liu, K., Zhang, H.: Military named entity recognition based on domain adaptation embedding. Comput. Sci. **49**(01), 292–297 (2022)
7. Huang, M., Liu, J., Dai, Q.: Chinese nested named entity recognition integrating improved representation learning method. Modern Comput. **27**(34), 21–28 (2021)
8. Zhang, B., Liu, K., Wang, H., Li, M., et al.: Chinese named-entity recognition via self-attention mechanism and position-aware influence propagation embedding. Data Knowl. Eng. **139**, 101983 (2022)

9. Zhu, H., He, C., Fang, Y., Xiao, W.: Fine grained named entity recognition via seq2seq framework. IEEE Access **8**, 53953–53961 (2020)
10. Hou, Y.: Research on Information Extraction Technology in the Field of Music. South China University of Technology (2019)
11. Yang, X., Sun, L., Liu, M.L., Xiao, K.Y., Li, C., Dong, X.C.: Knowledge graph construction with BERT-BiLSTM-IDCNN-CRF and graph algorithms for metallogenic pattern discovery: a case study of pegmatite-type lithium deposits in China. Ore Geol. Rev. **179**, 106514 (2025)
12. Zhang, R.: Knowledge Graph Construction of Music Intangible Cultural Heritage. North China University of Water Resources and Electric Power (2024)
13. Pan, X.Q., Feng, Z.Q., Lu, Y., Zhao, L.F.: LGENER: a lattice-and GAN-based method for Chinese ethnic NER. Alex. Eng. J. **115**, 297–307 (2025)

Author Index

GPSR Compliance
The European Union's (EU) General Product Safety Regulation (GPSR) is a set
of rules that requires consumer products to be safe and our obligations to
ensure this.

If you have any concerns about our products, you can contact us on

ProductSafety@springernature.com

In case Publisher is established outside the EU, the EU authorized
representative is:

Springer Nature Customer Service Center GmbH
Europaplatz 3
69115 Heidelberg, Germany